LOST CHILDREN WHERE THE WILD THISTLES GROW

FREE YOURSELF TO FOCUS ON YOUR POSITIVES

A Novel Based on a True Story

Connie A. Thompson

LOST CHILDREN WHERE THE WILD THISTLES GROW
FREE YOURSELF TO FOCUS ON YOUR POSITIVES

Connie A. Thompson

ISBN: 9798335036269

Copyright 2024 Connie A. Thompson

All Rights Reserved.

All rights reserved. No part of this publication may be reproduced, distributed, or transmitted in any form or by any means, including photocopying, recording, or other electronic or mechanical methods, without the prior written permission from the author, except in the case of brief quotation embodied in critical reviews and certain other noncommercial uses permitted by copyright law.

First Printing; August 2024

Those wishing to connect with Connie A. Thompson, author of

LOST CHILDREN WHERE THE WILD THISTLES GROW

HOW HIGH DO CHIGGERS JUMP IN THIS MOMENT CALLED LIFE?

and *THERE ARE: NO SECRETS*

can visit her by email at **connieathompson01@gmail.com**

Dedicated to

Mary Ann – Love always and forever

My siblings – Free to live our best life; right now

The Durans – My parents who never changed their number

Anyone with a sibling – We each are finding our way; celebrating you

Table of Contents

Preface 1
Chapter 1: Called 5
Chapter 2: Mami's Instructions 9
Chapter 3: Elizabeth Marie 11
Chapter 4: Magdelina 21
Chapter 5: Real Insane—The Spirits 37
Chapter 6: Romando 47
Chapter 7: San Antonio 53
Chapter 8: Sandrida 61
Chapter 9: Sister Bond 67
Chapter 10: Francisco 71
Chapter 11: Sunshine Letter 77
Chapter 12: Come Back 83
Chapter 13: Papi Search 91
Chapter 14: Straight Talk 95
Chapter 15: Vino's Last Stand 107
Chapter 16: Tucson's Landing 115
Chapter 17: Magdelina's Salem 123
Chapter 18: Sister Chat 129
Chapter 19: Finally Free 135
About the Author 139

Preface

Long ago and what seems to be another lifetime, my future was vividly revealed to me more than once.

Almost similar in predictions, certain milestones the same yet stretched as far as the east is from the west, and distinctive, there were some unexpected twists that I didn't know could be negotiated with my God of this Universe. Still, it is my crazy story to disclose, and you better believe there are reasons why I have waited decades to share with the world various realities of my past.

It all came back in waves of invasion when I chose to return to my origins—my birth family in Austin, Texas. I had reconnected with my biological mom, who I call Mami (sounds like Mommy). Time with Mami had been spent sharing memories of my childhood, of which she would complete my stories, which were memories—both good and traumatic. Mami would then take me to the locations where my recollections had occurred. Mami had addressed some tough topics of physical, mental, emotional, and sexual abuse as well as neglect. There are no secrets when truths are exposed, and everything comes out into the open.

At some point during my fourteen-year span of visiting Mami several times a year, extensively interviewing her, and digging up truths about my history, I had gotten brave enough to ask her about happenings that were to me odd and some supernatural. Honestly, have you ever looked in a mirror and seen people, and none of them were you? Yet your heart knows, some are from the past, some are alive now, and some have yet to be born. Have you ever been able to tell one's future, and it came true? When working with "at risk" youth, have you ever been able to get them to trust you because you told them their deepest, darkest secret that they never shared with anyone, but you told them detail by detail what had happened? Have you ever sensed something evil and used meditation and prayed it away knowing only goodness can terminate wickedness? Have you ever said something out loud, and it happened, then been asked by those around you how you knew about it? Well, it appears that this is not normal, and I wanted to know where it came from and how to make it go away because I did not want any part of this phenomenon. Mami said she would answer my curiosity. In turn, I was to fulfill my destiny in this lifetime, even though I did not believe I should be the one to be held responsible for sharing our private family story with the world. Why did our narrative have to be for others to learn and grow from? Honestly, was she such a narcissist to believe anyone would want to know our personal chronicles?

One, it is an outlandish account that most people are not going to care about, let alone believe. Two, why do I wish to share such an account of hurt and heartbreak? Three, what is it to the world to know my business? Mami should know that I am a reserved person; she can tell the future, senses and feels truths of the present, and is often called an empath. She is known as a fortune teller. She can even look into your eyes and read your past. How in the world does one become so knowledgeable with such skills? Were they inborn or learned? Still, I had agreed to complete my "destiny" by succumbing to her supplications. To be released from my assigned providence and return to a life I would consider "normal," I was to bid her requests. My destiny was to find each of my siblings, learn their stories after that momentous, thundering, stormy night when we each were "snatched into the darkness," never to return to our childhood maltreatments. Mami had a message for me to deliver to each of her children to assist with their growth and progression onward in life. A word of truth to appease the soul and allow endurance in our present existence.

These few words will document my quest to locate my siblings, to share our stories, and to deliver Mami's message to each of her exquisite children.

So, if you are looking for an energizing experience that involves reconnecting with siblings and wish to know what that may look like, then hang on and grab this book. It will embrace the opportunity for you to "free yourself and focus on your positives."

Thus, we begin my tale.

Chapter 1

Called

That moment when life stood still. Flashed by the brightest sunbeam that I have ever experienced, blinded by an aura of seeing beyond the living instantaneously, spinning in the warmth of endless peace and comfort. Was this genuine? The depth of what I saw was infinite and all around me, yet here and now, in my laundry room, it was for a split second. Looking toward the direction of the kitchen, Constance caught sight of the clock; it was ten-eleven at night. What was going on? The only way to explain this moment is to think of a brilliant, intense, dazzling sunray bouncing off the chrome trim of a classic car. It seizes your vision immediately, so vividly and robustly, throwing you off balance for just a twinkling of an eye that snuffs your breath away. Shaken and in tears, there was only one explanation, and I dared not call anyone in my family to research the truth of my suspicion, so instead, I went for a thirty-minute walk. After the vigorous saunter through the neighborhood, I called my Texas best friend. I just had to talk to Marisa O'Connor-Breaux.

Marisa and I had been friends for over twenty years. Even though I was about fifteen years younger than she was, no one would ever know now. Back in 1992, I had been her boss at my first real professional job after graduating from Emporia State University. Marisa loved being quizzed by co-workers and other community agency representatives we worked with weekly, then turning to me and stating, "I don't know. Ask my boss." Whoever she was speaking with would look at me with a surprised glance, and Marisa would burst out laughing and simply walk away. After Marisa had obtained her master's degree and moved onto better financial opportunities, we stayed friends and, through the years, became more like sisters, choosing to go through life together. She lives in Kemah, Texas, and I reside in the Dallas-Fort Worth Metroplex or, as we say to each other, "just one phone call away." There is no one like Marisa; she chain-smokes out of boredom, drinks Jack Daniels like water, then swaps to her daily dose of brewed fresh coffee. She incessantly resembles a blue-eyed, blonde-haired angel with perfectly manicured nails. Marisa's sensuous and slender body appears considerably fit and nourished, which is mind-boggling since she never enters a gym; she just has a fast metabolism and the energy of three people combined. Marisa cooks like any top chef in the world, can sew and create anything from scratch, is the best "fix it yourself" handywoman that Constance knows, and, most of all, is just honest and genuine. She declares profanity like a sailor but has a pure heart of gold. Calling her now, I thought I was going to pass out. I just knew Marisa would know what to do.

"Connie Jo, slow down sweetheart. I can't even hear myself think to process what you are attempting to share with me! What the hell is going on with you? Baby, S T O P, listen to me, and do what I am asking you to do: breathe in deep for three seconds, then breathe out for six seconds. Then let's try again. Use your words to tell me what is going on. Whatever it is, we are going to get through this together."

Constance smiled weakly because her given name is Constance. However, Marisa had given her what she believed was a more fitting name, Connie Jo, and she was the only one Constance allowed to call her that. Constance spent the next fifteen minutes spitting out her qualms about this unexpected gut-wrenching, spiritually illuminating, ashen vision or whatever it was she just experienced.

Marisa was one of the very few who knew what Constance had endured the past ten years, causing her to be in financial ruins. She was dealing with medical issues that were extensive and a multitude of extensive adversities for her family, so much so that their future had been challenged to the point of demise. Constance's marriage was over, leaving her to begin her life all alone again.

Marisa's mom had recently passed and left a small inheritance to her. Constance could not believe her ears when Marisa was instructing Constance to go on her trip, that money was being wired to her today, and Angel Mom would have insisted Constance get part of the inheritance anyway, so not using her portion of the inheritance was not an option.

"Connie Jo, it will cover your round trip completely to include your airline ticket, and give you spending money for renting a vehicle, getting gas, and doing what you need to do for a week, so go and don't look back."

"I won't be able to pay you back for many years because I plan to pay my debt off in full, and that means at least a decade of seclusion and focusing on being debt-free."

"Connie Jo, Mom gave that money not so that you could repay it but because she left one final showing of her love for you, so honor her by accepting her gift. Besides, she would love knowing she was able to help you when you truly needed her."

Teary-eyed, Constance whispered, "Thank you, Marisa. I will call my boss as soon as I get off the phone with you and will leave in two days. I will keep you updated and let you know what is going on. I love you, and just can't thank you enough. I was not expecting this. You have given me the greatest gift in life, and I will forever be grateful."

"Connie Jo, money is nothing unless it goes to a good cause, and, well, you are worth more than what money can buy; never forget that. I love you, and you had better call me before you get on that plane out of Texas."

Chapter 2

Mami's Instructions

Many moons ago and not so far away, I had been internally guided to return to my past in Austin, Texas, to learn the history of what led to my adoption. Throughout my young adulthood, a span of fourteen years, I revisited repeatedly my birth family, particularly my momma, who I call Mami (pronounced "Mommy'), accumulating family information until one day, she told me that my time with her was fulfilled, and it would be the last time that she would ever see me. It would now be my destiny to search for and spend time with each of my siblings and reveal her messages to each, what she considered important details. Mami already knew in her heart that I was aware of where most of my siblings were located and stayed connected to them by mail and phone calls, but we rarely talked about the past. To us, it was too overwhelming to relive it, so we just focused on our adopted world and what was happening in our daily lives.

Mami wanted me to have conversations with my siblings about what they remembered from their Austin experiences. In turn, the information I had to offer from her would assist with their inner healing, the settling of their deepest trauma and piecing together their earlier period of existence. In doing so, each could move on with their existing life. Even more than that, each would have the knowledge to free themselves and to focus on their own positives; better lives is what the rest of their existences would be all about instead of what happened to them in the past.

The reality is four little girls and a baby boy were snatched in the middle of one thunderous night. We were called the "Lost Children." We were there, and then we disappeared from family, friends, and the neighborhood like we had never existed. In addition, Mami wanted me to share with the world about the children who were left behind—the ones that were never adopted.

Finally, there are the few reconnections with my abusers that I was to locate and give messages to as well. Truth be told, I mentally had to process this task through my spirit of deepest inner struggles because I was not convinced that I wanted to spend my energy associating with any of my historical abusers. Mami had already told me that I would complete everything in due time.

It is interesting how time naturally evolves and creates circumstances that lead you to be right where you need to be to complete what you are destined to finalize, regardless of your feelings and desire to run toward the opposite direction, far removed from what your fate has in store for you. So it will be what it will be. In the meantime, I will just live my daily life.

It was easy to start Mami's requests because all I had to do was begin with my favorite person in the world—my die-hard sidekick from childhood beginnings—my sister Elizabeth Marie. I began by contacting her, and instead of focusing on our adopted lives, I initiated with the past.

Chapter 3

Elizabeth Marie

My most beloved and favorite person in the world is my sister Elizabeth Marie. She is one year younger and filled with a zealous amusement for life and a never-ending humor that is infectious. She is one inch shorter than myself and often declares, "Don't think I won't catch up to you because I am still drinking my vitamin D and growing taller every single day!" I just love her to pieces. All her life, she has been teased because of her weight, but I just command people to back off and leave her alone. She suffers from a hereditary trait that does not allow her to lose weight like you and I do. I know that our birth father, Papi, and his youngest brother, also had the same condition. When I was in foster care, my uncle lived four houses down the street, and I remember asking him all sorts of questions about his health and trying to understand why, even though he walked a lot and had a strict diet, he was still unable to lose weight. I recall the day that he passed. It took the fire department to come and cut his double-wide bay window completely out just to carry him out of the house. Our uncle was only five feet nine inches tall but weighed almost six hundred and fifty pounds. His heart just couldn't keep up with the pressure of maintaining his daily bodily functions. Tio Simon was only forty-three when he died.

Back to this moment, it could also be that we were the most resourceful kids in our early childhood days prior to being removed permanently into the Texas state child protective system. A prime example was when we would wait until it rained and then collect water in cups, buckets, or any plastic bags that we could find. Even at the tender ages of four and five, we learned we could use this fresh source of rain for drinking, washing clothes, cleaning our bodies, and even cooling our foreheads if we were sick. We were the ones who would attempt to clean the house or collect and basically hoard food when we could. It was Elizabeth Marie and our youngest sister Sandrida, who had been trained by our godmother, who lived a few houses down the street, how to change a cloth diaper and reuse it on our youngest infant sibling, our brother Romando. We were also the two offspring who couldn't wait to go to school and learn whatever we were supposed to learn that day. We'd come home and compare notes with what we had learned from preschool and try to repeat some of the lessons at home just to practice. Mostly, we would use a tree branch as our writing tool and the dirt as our chalkboard. We spent hours attempting to memorize and sing our songs loudly so that we wouldn't forget our newly learned words.

Another task that took an enormous amount of time was making every effort to search the streets for money because Elizabeth Marie loved to eat Cheetos, Fritos chips, cigarette chewing gum, Chick-O-Sticks, pickles, and drinking Big Red soda, plus our favorite Mexican cookies. We spent countless hours searching the streets, laundry mats, and the floors at the neighborhood convenience stores to hopefully find a little pocket change. We would collect what we could then go and talk to our lady friend at the neighborhood convenience store. Her name was Ms. Dolores. The store was in the bottom half of a house. She and her husband owned it, and her family lived in the top half of the house. It was located only half a block over, in the direction of the laundry mat, and one block north from the railroad tracks near the pink house where we lived. Further northeast up the road was Interstate 35. We would ask her to see how much more we would need to get a treat or two. As an adult now, I understand that Ms. Dolores was the only reason we ever got treats because she would count the seven pennies that we had found, and miraculously, it would be enough for all the items we wanted. How I wish I could find her to thank her for all her goodness.

Elizabeth Marie was officially the first one out of all of us to be legally adopted. From the moment she went to be with her new family, she was the one who reached out and wrote to me first. She was nine, and I was ten. Letter after letter, she would write about her efforts to get her new parents to adopt our youngest sister, Sandrida. Daily, she would cry for them to bring Sandrida home so that Sandrida would not be alone in foster care. We would exchange accounts of our travels and adventures. Both my adopted family and hers traveled the United States often, and we would share our highlights about our exposure to cultures and activities we were discovering. Equally, she and I loved the beach and the desert sand dunes. Elizabeth Marie would giggle when I described traveling to many different states to exhibit our pedigree dogs: American Akitas, Labradors, and boxers, in prestigious dog shows that were often shown on television. We even had a few who traveled the world with their trainers and were considered champions in their breed, and often, we could locate them in books and articles about their own standard breed. "Constance," she would burst out snickering. "Your dogs are stunning and eat better than we did when we were little bitty kids. Who has that kind of money to ship their dogs around the world for dog shows? Did you see all the grooming they get and the food they eat? I would die for that kind of luxury."

But nothing was as exciting for us as the wonderful places our parents would take us out to eat. Cafes, restaurants, hot dog stands, farmers' markets; we shared all our fortunate experiences of such wonders of cookery and fine dining. The large amounts and variety of food that we were exposed to were truly grandiose. Being children who were malnourished at the beginning of life with limited exposure to the recommended daily allowance of healthy food groups, nothing compared to this blessing. So, Elizabeth Marie and I spent an enormous amount of time discussing recipes and the best ways to stretch our food and to never again run out of groceries and feel the excruciating pains of real hunger. Lord willing, we would never have to go through the desperation of searching for food in trash cans or the backs of grocery stores or beg for food from neighbors. It was interesting to us how a severe lack in childhood became our obsession with food to the point that we cut out photos of delicious meals from magazines to share with each other.

We would review and rate similar restaurants we ate at in our own states—I lived in Kansas, and she resided in Arizona. We even had a scale of one to four golden stars for the quality of fresh fruit and vegetables and even the method in which they were prepared, especially those new foods we had never had before, such as ugli fruit or eggplant. Another example would be taking a banana and maybe today it would be baked with chocolate, sprinkled with a buttery Graham Cracker crust and a drizzle of caramel or dipping a banana in chocolate and covering it with nuts and diced strawberries, then freezing it or making a peanut butter and banana smoothie with yogurt, milk, and honey. Honestly, our passion for cuisine was insane.

Elizabeth Marie loved food almost as much as she loved her dramatic sitcoms and movies. In her Spanish world, her focus was her comedy dramas called Novellas in Spanish. "Constance, we can ONLY talk for ten minutes today because, you know, my novella *Ugly Betty* will come on, and I must go and see what is going on with my girl Betty. Honestly, I wish you would watch it so that we can compare notes and explore our thoughts on what will happen next. It is the life I want to live, the way I want to fall in love, and yeah, I know I am already married and have my child, but you know what I mean. In my romantic world, this is the way my life would go."

Through the years, every week with my lovely sister has been filled with laughter and amusement, always planning how we are saving up money to see each other. Each time we visit on the phone, we discuss how much love she has for her child, Annabeth Marie, ways to make a higher income so that we can meet somewhere more often, food ideas, and low-cost activities to do so that we can experience life to the fullest. We would also have dialogue on our love for our Heavenly Father

God, who spared us from worse pain than we had already experienced in our youngest years of life, and just telling each other we love each other and we are so grateful we escaped any further childhood pain just in the nick of time. We are the lucky ones because some never get the opportunity to have a second chance at a better life. Yes, we are so blessed. Every week, even to this day, we connect just to hear ourselves breathe in and exhale, sharing the goodness of what life gives us now. Elizabeth Marie and I love to hear each other over the phone, sharing with one another our love for each other and thinking out loud about anything that comes to mind. There isn't a topic too small to ruminate. Elizabeth Marie and I are truly best friends!

The first time that we reconnected in person was when we were both in our early twenties. Elizabeth Marie had been working every weekend, volunteering for overtime, plus worked her summers from the minute she got her first job at the age of sixteen to save up enough money to come to Texas and see Mami for herself. She didn't just wish to come for a weekend but to stay a few months and really enmesh her world with Mami's.

She had called me to ask me to meet her in Austin for a very long weekend, and we would explore Austin together. She wanted to see and know everything I knew. Plus, she wanted to meet any people that I had already reconnected with so that she would know who I was speaking of when I told stories about our family and friends in Austin and surrounding cities. I even introduced her to my foster parents, and she couldn't believe how near we were to each other, just two streets over. We had even gone to the same drive-in movie theater and didn't even know it. Her foster care experience had been hell on earth, and she would never ever wish to see any of those families ever again, but that's another story for another time. We never knew that we were so close in proximity during our foster care years or we would have seen each other more often.

The weekend finally arrived, and when we first glanced at each other, we could not stop staring, laughing, crying, talking, gazing, and hugging each other. Elizabeth Marie kept exclaiming, "Do you color your hair? It used to be more reddish brown, and now it is a light black!"

Laughing, I remember telling her that my hair had evolved and gotten darker the older that I got, so yes, it went from auburn to almost black. It was an incredible moment filled with authentic bliss; we were so caught up with each other that it took a while to realize others were near us, just watching our reunion. Everyone was crying and taking photos. Yes, it was surreal.

We spent every waking moment with Mami and explored our old neighborhood. I acted as the tour guide; Mami shared details and answered any specific questions that I was unclear on, and we conversed until we fell asleep anywhere we were at. At times, it would be at the dinner table, other times on the couch, in our sleeping bags, outside on the porch on Mami's favorite "old timey" rocking chairs; it did not matter because we were together. As we did when we were children, we would hold hands and hug a lot, not believing in our good fortune, that in this lifetime, we would be able to be together again. Our love for one another, no one will ever understand because we went into the pits of hell together repeatedly. Yet here we are on this side of early adulthood, speaking with one another in the flesh. How lucky we are to be in each other's company, enjoying precious time as one. Life is good at this moment. What an astonishing, wondrous period, and neither one of us ever wanted to let go. We held hands; we hugged, touched each other's faces, measured and compared our heights, and were awed at how similar in shape our hands were to one another, except Elizabeth Marie's hands were smaller. The best part was being face-to-face, sharing photos of us through the years in our adopted homes. Even though we knew each other's stories from all our growing-up conversations and correspondence, we still discussed every detail with each photo available before us. How we loved and missed each other so much.

Then we skipped down the path that was a half a block away to the house/convenience store we used to visit as children.

"My god," Elizabeth Marie and I both squealed at the same time because coming straight toward us was Ms. Dolores herself.

We ran to her and hugged her as she yelled for her husband to come to see the little girls, grown-ups now, who used to come and buy from them when they were little. Today, Constance pulled out a hundred-dollar bill and told Ms. Dolores that they were going to spend the whole thing here at her store. Ms. Dolores laughed and stepped behind the counter to pull out our favorite Mexican yellow cookies with the pink sugar dust on the top and two of the large molasses bread cookies shaped as pigs that just melted in our mouths. *Wow, still such a thoughtful, nice lady.* Constance prayed for a quick blessing over such a kind human angel. Both Elizabeth Marie and Constance picked out a bag of goodies worth a hundred dollars, then hugged Ms. Dolores goodbye, before leaving their happy hideaway from their past. It was such a warm fuzzy feeling that Constance did not want to let the moment go. She would file this moment deep in her mind for later and write about it one day. How unbelievable is the goodness of people who truly care about preserving the innocence of children and giving them hope when there are only hints of connections to impact their futures?

At one of the visits that Constance had completed here in Austin, she had spent time with Ms. Dolores and had found out she was one of the adults who had called child protective services on several occasions and the police to come and check on the children who were left alone to fend for themselves for weeks on end. Ms. Dolores had told her she worried someone would kidnap us because we were on the streets without adult supervision way too often. On a weekly basis, she would cry, pray, and worry about us and our siblings, knowing it was not right that we were neglected, in her opinion. She would get frustrated because it was taking so long for the state to take us away permanently. Every time she would see us returned from foster care, she would tell her husband that she couldn't believe they would keep putting us in harm's way just because Mami would complete her plan of expectations to get her children back. Everyone knew it would just be a matter of time before they would take us away again because we were several children under the age of seven raising ourselves. Worst case scenario, we'd be in the news for being kidnapped from the neighborhood or dead on the street somewhere. Ms. Dolores would proclaim to her husband that if a child came up missing or dead when the state should not have returned us to begin with, she was going to sue the state for negligence.

What really caught Constance off guard was when Ms. Dolores shared that she couldn't have her own children and how she and her husband wanted so badly to adopt us. However, our family was so well-known in Austin and surrounding cities that it would be an impossible thing to do and be able to stay in the neighborhood because they were sure a family member would come and take us away. Constance was delighted to have spent time with Ms. Dolores because she confirmed what a child's memory cried out. "I was abused and neglected yet spared of such heartache and permanent wretched demise."

There were those in the neighborhood who did care, but their hands were tied, and all they could do was report the abuse and hope the authorities would take us away permanently one day.

The long weekend with Elizabeth Marie went by too quickly but we both knew we would meet up again, and each time we would dig a little more, but for this time, it was just reminiscing, fun, and an unforgettable stretch of time spent together. We pinky swore and promised each other we would make the effort to see one another several times and more in our lifetime—no matter what—because we knew it was our destiny.

As I was getting ready to drive away, Elizabeth Marie spoke softly. "Next time, we will discuss our gifts and compare."

"What gifts?" I wanted to know what she was talking about. "Elizabeth Marie, honestly, you know I will be calling you, and we will discuss it over the phone because I can't wait until we meet in person to converse on this subject."

Driving home, I had a lot to think about, but first, I knew it was time to get ahold of my oldest sister, Magdelina, and chatter about more than our usual adopted family's itineraries, personal goals, and achievements. For us, it was never a competition to see who had better, but our way of making sure we kept in touch and felt like we were connected. We had been in foster care together for years and seen a lot we could never unsee. The next couple of hours were spent speaking with Magdelina on the phone. I told her all about my time spent with Elizabeth Marie and Mami. We spent the next two hours going over every little detail, ruminating, and analyzing every thought. It was a good ride home.

Chapter 4

Magdelina

Constance knew she would always be connected to her older sister, Magdelina, from the day they were all taken to their new homes. Constance went to Wichita, Kansas, and Magdelina headed to Hershey, Pennsylvania "like the candy bar" Magdelina would explain her hometown name. We were able to write to each other and talk on the phone with one another through the years.

Constance and Magdelina had the same child protective services social worker, whose name was Georgia-Lynn. She had explained to them that all the parents of our siblings had granted authorization, which allowed the picnic occasion to occur and for us all to spend time together. You see, it was an event put on by all our assigned private agency and state social workers, visiting caseworkers, CASA advocates, and the Foster Care Supervisor. It was an affair meant for interaction that was intentionally set up so all these workers could observe how the families would mingle among each other. If, at any time, anything did not network in a positive way, then the adoption process would not move forward for a particular family of a certain child.

Even though the birth family reunification plan had ended, it was the desire of all involved for siblings to remain connected. In our case, every family passed, and we all were allowed to travel with our designated new relatives except for Sandrida, who did not have a chosen adoption family match to date. This picnic event took place in early 1979. I was nine years old and would turn ten that summer. Magdelina was eleven, and she would have a birthday in the summer as well.

Throughout the years, we have kept in contact through letters and phone calls, covering our developmental growth into adulthood and our love for life. Each letter was a document of one another's: hobbies, activities, travels, foods we were introduced to, school experiences, adopted family lifestyles, church activities and beliefs, and typical girl phases of development. We discussed our favorite music, styles of clothing we were wearing, current hairstyles, our body types, and ways to stay fit, sports, and extracurricular activities we were in. We were generally interested in who was taller and who had the lighter brown eyes with our genetic blue ring around the brown. As we grew older, we talked about our dating experiences and living independently in the "real world."

When Constance returned to Austin, Texas, to their family origins, there were some conversations on birth genetic curiosities such as "Who do we look like, why did we have a blue circle around our eyes because some had hazel and blue eyes, and where did all the respiratory issues come from?"

Most Mexicans have brown eyes and dark hair, and we children did not. We also wanted to know who remembered us and were the schools, local bakeries, and churches that we recalled still there? Magdelina was continually asking for photos of when we were little. This was a daunting task because not even our social workers had been able to locate photos of us younger than six and eight years old.

Magdelina and I were the two sisters kept together in foster care, with four years being the longest we stayed at any one foster home. So, finding infant and toddler photos was like searching for gold under rocks; just not happening. When Magdelina had her first child, she longed for baby pictures of us, and through all the years of research,

Mami was only able to produce one photo. It had cost Constance over three hundred dollars to restore the photo, but it was theirs to have and well worth the price. Constance was ten months of age in the photo, and Magdelina was eighteen months older. Both recalled the image so vividly because it hung on the wall near the large record player wooden sound system in the living room of the pink house with Mami's other favorite photos of her father and her family when she was young.

They discovered when they were on the phone that, as they aged, they sounded so much alike and had similar laughs. They would giggle and observe something weird, like they were talking to themselves on the phone, but it was really each other's voices that sounded alike.

Constance was always intrigued but never questioned Magdelina when she told her that she, under no circumstances, wanted to speak about the bad things they had gone through as children because that was behind her. After having her own child, she decided she was a very private person, and she wanted her past pain and all her darkest moments of horror kept there behind us. Constance would sigh and gently state, "Magdelina, I was there, too, I know what happened, and I hurt and suffered also, even though we don't discuss details. I will write about it one day, and you can tell me what you think then."

She strongly stated, "No, I did all that therapy stuff, talking with counselors and my parents, when I was first adopted. I never wish to mentally repeat those memories out loud again. So, no, you can count me out having any further conversation about our painful past ever again in this lifetime. Sorry, sister, I just can't speak about it ever again. It is over and in the background of my head. You know, I just want to live in the moment and raise my children."

Magdelina stood at five feet even, and if she weighed one hundred pounds, I would be surprised. She always looks like she has just spent a long weekend tanning at the beach. I am almost three inches taller than her, and except for being lighter in complexion, we have similar features, and there is no denying we are sisters. Her hair is straight as a board and long, well past her waist, and mine is almost black with auburn highlights and curly.

She has a reputation for being very quiet until you get to know her, then she is a firecracker, purely stubborn with a very intense personality. Her eyes will pierce you like a knife, with nothing getting past her. She, too, has the gift of seeing beyond the living and understanding long before others do. She is decisive with her opinions and stands up for anything she considers worthy and good. It is difficult to gain her trust, but if you do, you will have a friend for life. Her life is not without struggles, but she pushes forward and believes her children to be strong, smart, loving, and independent.

Magdelina ended up having two incredibly stunning girls that she adores and wants the best for them, even though she feels she was almost too tough on them for a reason. She never wanted them to go through what we did as children, and she wanted them to be strong—to be able to deal with life that can be hard at times. She struggles with keeping employment because she cannot stand stupidity and has little patience for any nonsense. She prefers to keep to herself and through much therapy, she has learned her limitations. In the end, she is unable to work and is always dealing with the haunting of her past, which were so many beatings; often leaving her body, especially her backside, with scars. These mark memories of painful gutted skin and cuts that would often expose raw meat. She does not sleep well through the night, is on medication for her impromptu reactions, and has learned she does better with nature. Magdelina enjoys being around birds, trees, and the beach. The only thing that soothes her soul more is being around her children, who she loves beyond her own life and who she is incredibly proud of. Her bygone life has kept her from being nurturing and doting, like Elizabeth Marie and I seem to be—very hands-on, pampering, and extremely affectionate. She shows love by protecting her children and keeping them in her heart. She loves deeply and cares about both beyond words. She, like me, holds back and may have trust issues, but mostly because everything we love gets taken from us or is gone too soon. This makes us hesitate and withdraw within ourselves, leaving us as watchers and prayer warriors for those we love the most.

It isn't that we don't care; it's that we care too much and do not wish to go through the grief of intense loss if something should happen to our loved ones.

It would not be until decades later, when Constance published the fictional memoir *There Are: No Secrets,* that Magdelina would call her more than usual, weekly, just to discuss the book. This happened for years. Constance's diary-turned-fiction included conversations she had with their birth Mami condensing fourteen years of research to answer the question of what happened that they all came to be adopted.

If we came from such a stable and wonderful family known in the Austin community, then what happened to our nuclear family that there was so much turmoil and dysfunction to the extent that we were removed permanently from the family?

Constance would share her memories with Mami, who, in turn, would share her side of the story, then she would physically take Constance to the location where the memories originally transpired, and they would process Constance's feelings and additional questions. At the time, it was intense and healing, with some incredibly tough sessions of interrogation and built-up emotions that were passionately expressed toward Mami. Mami was just as penetrating, sharing her side of her story and letting out her hurt from the past: her regrets and disappointments. Yet Mami was able to express her train of thought to release her children permanently because her love outweighed her need to have us all with her. Her desire to protect her children by letting go was her only option and her last attempt to show each child that she loved them beyond belief, and she would never quit caring and praying for each one of us even beyond the living.

Magdelina: "Constance, I never knew what you went through. Yes, we were together in the same house, but I was so caught up surviving in my own world, thinking I was alone, I never considered what any of you were going through. My body never had to withstand cigarette burns or razor cuts. You understand what I went through better than anyone else I know. Mine were mostly beatings, with my backside being so cut into, gashed open with such painful rawness that I would get into trouble at school for not wanting to sit down or lean back on a chair. Then, when they checked me at the nurse's office and, of course, they saw why I could not sit, they had to call child protective services. You get my past—the words I never wanted to say out loud, you wrote some of them in your book."

A deep nostalgic silence, knowing we were both transported to those moments of maltreatment, each in our own depth of pain. Somehow, these moments heal our past by embracing our pain together. Interesting how this could be accomplished over the phone yet allow space so that we could process these memories in our own way. There were so many unfathomable and excruciating incidents in our past that were just that—too much for any child to live through, and we both knew how fortunate we were to survive. We still can't believe Magdelina lived through the barbwire episodes without getting poisoned or needing more tetanus shots. We both wept: for each other, for ourselves, for our siblings, for the unfortunate fate of our family, for Mami having to make a choice no parent should have to make, for how it has affected our lives even though we have moved on and most of all for that dent in our history that should have never been. Now comforted, we are not alone in our depths of mixed emotions, and we have never been because we have a witness—we have each other.

Magdelina said it best. "Constance, you already know what hurts the most without me ever saying it out loud. I can share as much as possible and still others who don't get it, but you can read in between the lines and know the whole truth. I guess that is why God kept us together, even after all these years. I hope we see each other before we die because we are not getting any younger."

Through the years, something has always happened financially, medically, or just timing, and we have not ever been able to reconnect in person. The time will come when it is time to see each other in person. Our whole beings ache to see each other in person. Constance knows from Mami that the spells cast on her children come to an end when we see one another in person: our back and forth of restlessness and constant recycling of negative memories come to an end when we hug at our reconnection. Mami foretold our visit, and Constance knows it is near.

Mami predicted that we would not get to see each other until after I was over fifty. It just doesn't seem fair, but it's true—something has always made it impossible to complete this desire to see one another again. So I decided to share Mami's message over the phone. It was time for Magdelina to finish processing her healing so that she could sleep soundly at night, even though I know fate has it that she won't sleep soundly and fully until we see each other in person. Magdelina is way overdue, simply enjoying living in the moments of today.

"Magdelina, if I tell you something, promise not to freak out or get mad?"

"Huh, what are you talking about, and why would I freak out?"

"Well, do you remember when we were little, and we would talk to the spirits and tell the future, and stuff would come true? We both saw the dead, but they spoke to me, yet we were never scared. Just like gazing into the deep dark skies, we knew our destiny was written in the heavens, and everything is connected. The skies tell the human story and can guide us if we are willing to learn and use its wisdom to seek our destinies. We never feared. It was what it was."

"Uh yeah, but I thought only I understood that and saw those things. I honestly didn't understand that stuff until I got older, but yes, I remember."

"Well, Mami left you a message so that you can know that you are forever protected, loved, and can live a good life, and it is okay to be okay. But first, tell me this: What was it like for you to have an abortion?"

Magdelina gasped. "What did you just say? Constance, not even my parents know that information. I have kept that as my only deep dark secret all these years. Something extremely powerful and hurtful. A painful decision that I had to make when I was very young. To this day, I never forget my baby."

"Mami's message to you is, 'Magdelina, my wanted and beautiful child, these words I say to you. When you were born, it was one of the happiest days of my life. Such a gorgeous baby girl. You were an observant infant who loved to laugh. You were quiet, never missed a thing, and learned quickly. You potty-trained easily and walked earlier than your older sibling. You insisted on being on the go, always ready to leave the house. I had visions of your life being better and different than my own existence. Seeing the future, I know it to be true because another loving family would raise you and give you a world that I could not give you. Because my affection for you is deeper than the beginning of time, I could only choose to let you go and accept your destiny. That is my true love for you: letting go. May you know that my devotion to you is beyond the stars in the depths of our universe. Forever remember and know that you deserve what I could not provide for you and your siblings. It is not what I wanted, but it was the best for you. When you hear this message, I will be long gone, but you need to be aware, your little boy, that you had to make a tough choice and let go. He is in heaven, and he is with me. He is healthy and whole. I am with him, and it is good. He watches over you and knows you love him and care about him, never forgetting him. In heaven, there isn't any sorrow, so discern with your heart you will see him again, and when you do, it will be as it always should have been. When you see a cardinal or a blue bird, know it is him nearby, loving you, always adoring you, his beautiful and wonderful Mommy. Magdelina, forgive yourself for the tough choice you had to make and take comfort in knowing your son; he loves you and worships you.'"

"Constance, how did you know? I have not ever told a soul."

"Magdelina, I don't know anything, just repeating what she told me to tell you."

"Damn. I have so many questions for her and wish she was here to answer them. I am at a loss for words. You know I hated her so much because she was never around and when she was, she did absolutely nothing. Just kissed ass and did whatever that grandmother woman made her do."

"Magdelina, what you don't know is that Mami took a lot of beatings for us so that we wouldn't have to be hurt so much. Then she would go away angry and hurt. Because her mother's black magic was so real, they all feared what she might conjure up, possibly making our situation worse than just going through whatever we were going through at the time. It was when Mami started practicing and casting her own spells and choosing goodness to override our grandmother's evil curses that the battle was won. In exchange for saving her own children, Mami always told me that the price was an early death, but to protect us, she was ready to pay the price. May her soul rest in peace. Do you realize that she never saw age fifty-four?"

"Why didn't they just beat that hateful woman into leaving us alone? I refuse to consider her as our grandmother. She is nothing but evil."

Mustering strength, Constance murmured, "Magdelina, through the years, I have learned that our grandmother was raped by her brother and had his baby. It is the main reason she turned to alcohol and violence and, worst of all, her voodoo. She often chose the dark side to make everyone pay for her grief and lot in life. She pretty much had to go away to Austin, Texas, and marry our grandfather, who was twenty-seven years older than her, so that her baby would have a father, or she would be shaming her family. It was what they did back in the day. So, she left the comfort of the family ranch and went away to start a new life in the big city of Austin, Texas. But she brought her craft with her, and her own children feared the hexes she would cast, so they did whatever she asked them to do."

"I don't care that she was raped. She had no right to abuse us and be so cruel to us. We were children, and we never did anything to her."

"I know. She used to put me in a tub of ice-cold water up to my neck with bags of ice added to the water and tell me I was a bad girl because her brothers and cousins would molest me. She would always blame me. According to her, it was my fault that they would touch me when she wasn't looking. I remember one time getting so sick with fever after what seemed like hours and hours of exposure to the ice-cold water. My body would turn beet red with a painful burning sensation. I'd almost faint. I would be so miserable I couldn't talk or even think. Worse, she would not let me go to school in case someone said something about my skin. Yes, I know and experienced firsthand her brutality to us, but for my own sanity and sake, I forgave her long ago. Again, her abuse did not make it alright for her to hurt us. Magdelina, I am so grateful all of her abuse is in the past."

In an elevated screeching voice, Magdelina is bringing up so much pent-up rage. "I refuse to ever forgive her. She doesn't deserve it, not even in death! There isn't a hell hot enough to punish her for all the evil things she did and the pain she inflicted on us. Today, I am an adult and have found my voice. If she were here, I would tell it to her face! I am not scared of her voodoo and spells. My parents taught me I have a right to my feelings and my voice and damn it, I will use it forever, and I will never forgive her evil brutality."

I was trying to soothe Magdelina. I said in a gentle voice, "Because you were so smart and quick, our grandmother was never patient with you. She treated you much older than you were. She was physically abusive to her own children and even more so with her grandchildren. Occasionally, she had moments of goodness: cooking for us, sewing us clothes, taking us to Austin museums, bakeries near her pink house, and visiting the San Antonio, Texas farmer's market. Do you recall going to the farmer's market? Then, she would take us to get her stuff for her spells. Do you remember and envision those chilling moments with her? To me, they are 'flashes of time' that never go away, and that feeling of intense mystery about the world beyond that somehow lingers in the back of my mind. We do not war against ourselves but against the principalities of this universe, and I learned long ago to withdraw and let my higher power fight my fight. That holy spiritual world is incredibly real and powerful for me to want to be a part of and I admit it, I am fearful of its sovereignty capabilities. I want nothing to do with it."

"Yes, I remember. You know, Constance, every day, there is this huge crow that flies down and sits near me or circles around me anywhere I may be walking or sitting; I know that it is symbolic for her. I can sense her. Yes, I know she wants my forgiveness, but I refuse to forgive her. I will not allow it. In death, she should be restless and always searching for forgiveness and never find it. She does not scare me, nor do any of the dead that come to me and want us to know they walk among us until that day the God of this universe brings us all together and restores all things to the original plan; I don't fear any of them. You know, all they wish to do is communicate with the living for whatever reason, but her, well, I will not ever give her the satisfaction of my forgiveness. Fuck her. Death is eternal. May she rot in her own misery endlessly! My parents taught me long ago that these are my feelings, and I have the right to have them."

"Magdelina, I am so sorry for all the damage and harm you suffered. Because I was there, I saw how she was so much harsher with you than anyone else. I did find out later the reason she chose you as a scapegoat was because you looked exactly like her when she was little. She wanted to make you go away. She wanted to die but never had the courage to finish it. She had tried to take her own life many times. Instead, she chose alcoholism as a slow death. Magdelina, truth be told, our grandmother died a very painful death. It made the newspapers, and it matched the details Uncle Vino shared with me when I asked whatever happened to her. He was the one who heard her penetrating, deathly screams for help one summer morning at the ranch, just outside her second house. She always kept her house in Austin for her kids to have a home, but this house in Hill Country, well, that was her coveted home, her safety personal comfort, and she never gave it up. Her dad willed it to her just as he left a house to each of his children. Deep in Hill Country, where the wild thistles grow.

"She had just gotten the fire going outside because there was not any electricity at her residence. Each day, she would gather the wood and start a fire in the wee hours of the morning. She would then make coffee, hot water for bathing, and begin a large pot of stew, which would feed many. Then, the breads, tortillas, rice, and vegetables would be made in the man-made brick oven, also located outside. You could see her skinning a snake, chopping up cacti, and even wringing the necks of chickens if you got up early enough. On this day, she was making tortilla soup with chicken. Every vegetable, legume, herb, and fruit in the soup had come from her garden located on the other side of her house. What was amazing is that her house was less than six hundred square feet, and it housed large quantities of stuff she said she needed for her spells, gifts for visitors, and fabrics and materials for her sewing and crafting that she loved so much. Anyway, the dress she had on was very old and thin. It was made of cotton.

"Tio Vino told me, 'She spun around quickly when she heard me coming up the road from Aunt Patsy's house and then the screams. Her dress had caught fire, and it quickly consumed her. I ran to get a blanket and came back to wrap her in it and roll her on the ground. I got the flames to go out, but when I yelled for help, no one came, so I had to run to my aunt's shack to call the ambulance. I knew in my heart she wasn't going to make it. All her years of meanness and hateful ways … I forgave her in an instant and told her so. I tried to comfort her and soothe her. It didn't take long for help to arrive. I could hear a helicopter near and loud. Because the ranch is in the middle of nowhere, she was airlifted to the nearest burns unit. She died that same day. She was far too gone. She tried to fight, but she was too far gone. You know, in our family, those who have the gift and practice are doomed to die by fire or by water. She died by fire, and it was such a painful way to go. I will never get over seeing death by fire, especially when it was my own mother.'

"Magdelina, that was what Tio Vino told me of her story on how she died. I later researched it and found the newspaper article on her death. I will give you a copy of it when I can find the newspaper clipping."

"I am so glad she suffered, and I know that it is unkind for me to feel that way, but I don't care, she should have never hurt her own children and grandchildren. We were defenseless. She deserved a painful death, and if she were here, I'd say it to her face."

Constance sighed. "Don't you see, Magdelina? You are free to be free. You are free to focus on your positives. All of those who hurt us as children; each one of them is dead and gone. They can't ever harm us again. We have been set free to live a good life. There is no one in the shadows waiting to hurt us ever again. Set your mind loose and live life fully!"

"I see what you are saying, and I get it, but I am never going to forgive that woman. I hate her and what she did to me, and I detest that all other adults were too afraid of her casting spells to ever do anything about saving us from harm. I do, however, want you to know, my baby, I always believed him to be a boy, and I am in awe Mami even knew anything. Yeah, I believe in telling the future, but this truly confirms our spirituality with the universe is real, and there is life beyond this earthly living. You know, I already know that, but now this is one more thing to confirm it. Wow, just wow. Constance, do you ever really stop and think how lucky we were to have been snatched that dark, thundering night, never to return to our past and be given a new life? We are truly the lucky ones to go through what we did and live to talk about it. Isn't it crazy that we made it out?"

"Sister, we are blessed, loved, and in a good place to do anything we wish to do. Yes. For being known as the lost children where the wild thistles grow where no one can hear our agonizing cries to being snatched from evil. Yes, we are lucky! Magdelina, next time we talk, let's see what we can remember about the witchcraft, medicine woman stuff that has to do with our family, okay? I am too sleepy to think about it now."

"Aha, Constance, that stuff never goes away. I have just put it away in my head because, over time, I have learned it is not normal in every family I have met and were happenings that never occurred in my adopted family and my dad knew everything. He is scholarly and experienced, and the events we saw as children never happened anywhere else in my home, and we traveled around the world. I agree. Let's see if we remember the same stuff. I love you. Good night."

"Thank you, Magdelina. I'm glad you shared your side of your story, and I'm so saddened by all the pain you endured. I am sorry. You know, I appreciate you sharing what you have thought all these years, and I'm so glad we have an understanding. I love you. Magdelina, my beautiful, soulful sister, take this to your dreams tonight. Mami's final words to you: she wanted you to know you are free. 'Release and liberate your mind from your grandmother's cruelty. God does not like ugly, and in the end, He does bring justice. She cannot ever harm anyone again. Free yourself to focus on your positives. Magdelina, move forward, knowing her painful death brought an end to the witchcraft and abuse that got out of control. You live life to the fullest, never look back, and find your peace, your laughter, seeking goodness and joy. When you see this in print and realize the finality of those evil days gone by, then you will be able to rest through the night and truly have new beginnings. A beautiful, courageous child, you are genuine, innocent, pure, loyal, and forever loved. May the remainder of your long life be peaceful and filled with vivaciousness. Give your mind and body permission to rest and rejuvenate.

"Remember this, when you see Constance face-to-face and she releases you from your purpose as a child, then your unconscious shall be troubled no more, and you will sleep like you have never slept before—the kind of deep slumber that one experiences with tranquility.'

"Magdelina, your purpose as the oldest sibling was to draw attention. You accomplished that often by running away at the age of five and stirring up fights. You also reacted to anyone who would listen. This caused people to come and search and then they would find children who needed help. You were a saving grace to your younger siblings. Because of you, us kids were removed sooner. Because of you, you kept the rest of the children safe. Those days are long gone, and your purpose is no longer needed, so child, take care of you and rest. Just be still, quiet, and enjoy daily living. Give yourself permission to free yourself to focus on your positives. You are forever treasured and loved."

My eyes are like waterfalls, and my older sister is in silent reverence. This felt like being motionless for hours, but in truth, it was only a few minutes. Muttering, "I love you, Constance, thank you for this and for sharing Mami's words. I never knew. I am going to my room to rest and think about everything we have spoken of. I need to sort it all out in my head. Just know I am grateful we are sisters, no matter what we have endured. We are strong and have a purpose, even if others don't understand what that may mean. Our purpose was to survive, share, and give hope to others. We will speak soon again."

Our conversation was fruitful, therapeutic, and cleansing. It was good. We, the lost children where the wild thistles grow, weren't so lost after all. Rightly, we were set free all along when Mami let go long ago to be adopted and raised by those who could help us move forward in life. We must look inward, look up, and out to embrace who we truly are and free ourselves to focus on our positives.

Chapter 5

Real Insane—The Spirits

Elizabeth Marie called me one Friday evening squealing, "Constance, when are you going to tell me that you got a divorce? I already know you don't believe in divorce, but your marriage has been over since it started—all lies—but I insist you chatter with me."

"Honestly, Elizabeth Marie, between you and Mami, you exhaust me. I can't hide anything from you, and I can't keep my shit private. Tell me what this is all about, and don't make it about me because I also know that the man you call husband is abusing you, and you have lost a baby because of him, and you are still with him because you don't believe in divorce, so tell me, when are you going to stop allowing him to beat you up and send him back to Mexico where he belongs? Quit trying to help a useless piece of shit become an American; he is not a good husband, and you already know that he is using you to stay here."

Oh crap, I had gone too far. I had hit a nerve. Elizabeth Marie was crying and emotionally broken. "I am sorry, sweetheart, talk to me."

"Constance, I forget that you have the gift, too. You know stuff, and no one tells you about it—you just know. I just don't get why you don't want to practice your gift and make a business from it like our grandmother did?"

"Elizabeth Marie, I am sorry I hurt you, but you forget your honesty hurts me, too, and just because I allow you to tell me anything that you know, think, or feel does not mean that I am not crying on the inside wondering why you must expose my personal business."

"Okay, sister, I get it, and I will ask you in the future what your thoughts are if I know something about you. Do you want me to share what I believe is going on or going to happen to you, or do you just want to wait until you are ready to talk or allow fate to occur in your life?"

"Baby girl, I can't explain it. When you stir anger and frustration inside of me, that is when I just utter the truth. I had intuitive thoughts on how he treated you and sensed your husband was not genuine, but until just now, I honestly didn't know it was true until you started crying, and I knew that I hit a nerve and touched the exactness of what is going on with you. So, to be fair, you share what you wish to share, and know that my concern is your safety and happiness. In my heart, I feel that he killed your unborn child, and that is why you miscarried, even though I am not supposed to know yet that you miscarried."

Again, Elizabeth Marie is sobbing. "Oh Constance, I should have told you, no excuse because we talk every week. I should have said something. I just wanted my marriage to be happy and good, but instead, it is, as you say. Also, I am divorcing him. I should be honest with you. He found a beautiful girlfriend and no longer needs my help getting into the country. He told me that my having a baby would tie him down to me, so that is why he had to get rid of the problem and leave. He really has been a shitty person all along and only sweet in the beginning because he desperately needed a place to stay and my help to become a citizen. You know, the dumb shit really thought that he would get this gorgeous forty-five hundred square foot house my parents left to me and Sandrida if he married me. But, when he found out he wasn't getting squat, well, he was ready to move on. Oh well. Glad I didn't have his kid because it would be a hot mess; his new girlfriend is hateful and messy. I am glad I am soon to be done with his manipulation and mean ways. Anyway, the reason I called is to ask you if you remember the weird stuff that happened when we were little? Did I imagine it, or was it real?"

"Which events are you talking about?"

"You know, when that man levitated in the air, was healed by our grandmother, and then she spread ashes all over him and said his dust was restored and he was a new creation. The Lord saw his wife's tears, and he will live to see his grandchildren. She gave him little bottles of herbs and wrote down words to tell himself and pray daily until the eternal Spirit of death comes back for him. It was to be after his tenth grandchild was born that his life would be transitioned to glory. At the time, back when we saw this, his kids were our age in preschool."

"My gosh, Elizabeth Marie, how in the world did you recall that occasion? Because I vaguely remember the couple coming with those men who carried him into the house for help. He was already dead and had been for days. Creepy, just thinking about it now."

"Sister, his oldest daughter was four, just like me, and it made me realize maybe we could pray and get our Papi some help so that he could come home too.

"I also remember them drying the tops of the cacti that came from Hill Country, and they would smoke it and drink the apple and peach moonshine they made from scratch. Then, they would store everything in the dark cellar in the ground at Hill Country, where the wild thistles grow. Constance, I don't even know what a wild thistle looks like, just that they always said it. I was so scared to go down there because bad things would happen to me when Grandmother would have me go help bring up the potatoes and other vegetables from the cellar. I hated Tio Vino and Tio Flaco; it was always the same ones who would hunt and hurt me."

Tears gushing now, like a raging, unstoppable roaring waterfall on a windy stormy night, Constance wept. "Elizabeth Marie, no. NO. Please tell me, not you, too. No! I thought it was only me and Magdelina who had to endure the pain of molestation, sexual abuse, and beatings. Please tell me that it was not you, too. You were only three. My God, why God? How could you allow this to happen to my baby sister? I hate you for allowing such a precious, beautiful child to be hurt! I can't stand the pain that my heart is feeling right this instant. I can't breathe. My chest so tight, surely I will die."

The anguishing pain engulfed me so deeply and thrusted a double-edged sword through my heart, I could hear myself gasping for air, drowning in sorrow in such a way that I didn't even recognize my bellowing howls.

Elizabeth Marie is crying as well. "Constance, when they would tickle me, it was because I was so ticklish, and they were trying to stop me from screaming from the pain. I hear you share your stories, but for me it was physical abuse. Do you remember when they told the preschool teachers at Chacon Elementary school that I was in the hospital due to pneumonia? Well, that was partly true. The rest that no one was told was they would hang me upside down with a tight rope on my left ankle, and one day, they left me hanging upside down too long, and my ankle got broken. That is how I ended up in the hospital for weeks, not pneumonia. To this day I walk with a slight limp and, like today, must use a cane to support myself because when the weather changes quickly or it gets cold and wet, I hurt like hell. I am reminded of those horrible days of the past. I can't ever seem to fully escape the torture of those recollections. Those recalls seem to follow me even in my slumber."

"My gosh, Elizabeth Marie. I never experienced any broken bones, and I just remember crying my heart out because you went to the hospital, and they took us away and put us in foster care again. We were sent to our great-auntie's house by the Colorado River. They called it Kinship Placement or something like that. I think, right now, I am going to vomit."

Immediately I dropped the phone and ran to the toilet and hurled, all the while tears just pouring. When I got back on the phone, I just whimpered and lamented, "I didn't know that you were touched or hurt in any kind of way. I just can't believe they got to you too. My heart hurts so much right now. I am on the brink of morbid lamentation. I fear I will fall into a deep snooze and not wake up from excruciating, tormented sorrow. This is too much to absorb. I just can't stand anyone hurting you, Elizabeth Marie. I want to claw their eyes out and just bestow hardship on those who hurt you. No wonder your PTSD is worse than anything that I have ever experienced. You can't stand being in public, you can't sleep through the night without strong pills, you have fibromyalgia, you have a heart condition, your hoarding continues to get worse as you age, you are stressed even when there is not anything going on. Honestly, baby girl, it is not healthy for you to have all this mess going on in your head. I am so disturbed by your experiences of the past. May the God of our souls ensure eternal damnation to those who placed their hands on you, and may they suffer beyond eternity. Cursed be the day of their birth, and may our God have vengeance on them if they are still alive. My sweet baby sister, this is when I wish we lived in the same city so you can just come over and be with me, and I can hold you and comfort you. I love you beyond words, and I miss you so much."

My spirit was weighed down and in deep mourning. I couldn't quit weeping. My whole body was shaking from crying, and then I heard her diminished voice.

In a very calming voice, Elizabeth Marie whispered, "Baby girl, it is alright. The Lord has heard our cry, and He made a way for us where there was none. He taught me to laugh again. He gave me a child that I desperately longed for. He loves us beyond belief, and He has been with each of us all along. He alone will right the wrong. He alone will restore and make it as it should have been. I love you, Constance, and I am so proud of us and how God has allowed us to stay in touch so that we do not travel this road called life alone. He chose you for me and me for you. We are one and the same mindset: the way we see the goodness that life has to offer and choose to embrace life today with joy and purpose. Never quit being you, and always know you are loved and have been made whole for a reason. Tell our story in your books, and in the end, your life will be blessed and restored. I love you always, and I love being your baby sister."

"Elizabeth Marie, when I asked Mami where all this incest and abusive ways came from, she told me that we are not supposed to know we are of the indigenous people. They will never tell us which tribe, and one day, I shall find out that over half of our bloodline is of an incredible people that have always been a part of this land and decent. Also, we must know that is where the real insane isn't so insane but is spirituality that has been passed down from generation to generation. Our line is tied to the shaman, the healing medicine tribe that hears and speaks with the dead. The Spirits are among us always. We must not speak our thoughts that are dark, lest they come true; only choose the good and the happy to voice aloud. What we say comes into existence. The spiritual world is enormously powerful, prevailing above and beyond humanity. This is why we must fear and respect the great "I AM" because such omnipotence and mightiness always was and forever shall be. May all the siblings never be together in a single space, because there is true strength in numbers. Always choose goodness, choose life, and decide to bless, give, and care.

"You know, Elizabeth Marie, I told Mami I wanted nothing to do with such hocus-pocus because if spirituality could not spare her own children from the deep hole of maltreatment and exploitation, then why in the hell would I want to claim and engross my efforts into some voodoo that can't even protect the innocent. No, thank you."

"My lovely sister, I adore you for being you, genuine, and allowing yourself to see and know the truth, but you are wrong about the spiritual world. This is the devil's earth until the return of our Lord, and we don't fight against flesh and blood but spiritual existence. That is why we must allow our God to fight our fight. The time will come when there will be justice and revenge, paid in full, and everything will be restored as it should have been to begin with. For now, may your peace come with knowing that we were given the opportunity to escape any further torture or abuse of our childhood. I just wish that I could turn it off in my head and let the nightmares go. I just can't, and I know that it will send me to an early grave one day, but not even therapy or strong medications help with turning off the memories that torment me daily."

"Baby girl, just tell me what I can do to ease your pain."

"Constance, finish all three books and allow your path to be restored; then and only then will you be able to assist my child. I wish for her to spend time with you in this lifetime, to know our past—the good parts—and you know our stories best. You can help her meet family and friends if she is ever curious and interested. You will need funds and time to make all that happen, so get to writing and don't look back. Also, next time we talk about the spirits, can you tell me about the San Antonio visits?"

"We shall pray for peace and strength to move forward and choose life. I love you. Yes, we can cover the San Antonio visits. Only Magdelina and I were allowed to make those voyages to the medicine men and mentors for our grandmother. Let's rest and talk again soon."

After we got off the phone, I ran to my bed and flung my body diagonally across the pastel green satin floral bedspread and wept until I fell asleep. The next day, I called in sick to work and sobbed until my body ached. This was healing somehow. It was time to release the past. Most of those who had harmed us were gone, and soon I would be facing Papi and Uncle Vino to confront and lay to rest what should never have been. Cleansed and exhausted, I slumbered into oblivion.

When I woke up, it was a little after noontime, and I knew I had to call Marisa.

Marisa answered the phone with her usual, "Connie Jo, I love you, and I am so glad you called."

"Oh Marisa, I just have to tell you something, and I know that you won't judge, but I need to hear your thoughts on what you think," and so I proceeded to tell her everything from my conversation with Elizabeth Marie from the day before.

"My God, I am so sorry to know what you and your sister experienced as children, and I wish I were there to hold you and comfort you. I am sorry that you hurt. I hear anguishing sorrow in your voice, and I know you want to take all the tortures your sister has endured, but sweetheart, we must all walk our own path and sort through our demons alone. We can be there to comfort and be good listeners who support through the process, but only we alone can work through our pain. Are you listening, Connie Jo? Because I know how your mind wanders, and this message you need to hear loud and clear. You, Connie Jo, must not carry the weight for Elizabeth Marie. You can be empathetic because if anyone knows what she has gone through, you know more than most.

"Connie Jo, listen to me and understand with your heart opened. You were children, and you were violated, and no adult on the inside of your world protected you when they should have. Parents who are responsible are there for their children, and apparently, you did not have active parenting that gave a shit enough to protect you. Constance, you were babies, and it was not your responsibility to be an adult, so do not carry that burden of guilt. Nothing you did could have changed the adult poor choices that were made. Do you comprehend what I am saying right now?"

Even though I absorb Marisa's words and internalize her truths, my heart is broken, and I just can't get over that. I just didn't know what was going on in the next room to the most important person in my life. To know how much Elizabeth Marie was violated just broke my soul.

"Marisa, I understand. It is just that I thought even as a child, if they were hurting me, surely they were not hurting my younger siblings and I was completely wrong. Why did I not think to ask Elizabeth Marie sooner about the past? I just don't know. I could have been comforting her sooner than now."

"What the fuck, Connie Jo. Quit being the caregiver and just focus on having a healthier relationship with Elizabeth Marie now. She is only one year younger than you and is an adult. Choose not to carry the weight of the world on your shoulders and teach yourself to back away from what is out of your control, or you will send yourself to an early grave. I am not ready for you to meet death, and only you can shut out and choose not to be accountable for what is out of your control. Got it? Connie Jo, I love you, but it is time you focus on your life—your wants and your needs. I understand you want to be there for Elizabeth Marie, but you are both in the same boat—bad things happened to you as children—and the past is over. Quit reliving it over and over in your head.

"It is time to hurt through the pain of what happened to you, grieve, and then learn new coping mechanisms to replace your unhealthy ones. Find out your triggers that send you into that deep dark cave of pity and self-doubt, and then work on them. Whether you see a counselor or tap into a support system, that is your choice, but find what works for you and process through the madness of the past so that you can enjoy the present and your tomorrows.

"You will know when your healing is real when you no longer seek to constantly help others, but instead, choose to help as you wish and see fit. Instead, you take care of yourself first, live in the now, and share your experiences. Constance, your past becomes stories to distribute with others to grow from and less of reliving it over and over. That is how you will know you have moved on from the past."

"I love you, Marisa, and, yes, like you said, the group that has helped the most is my support system, which has taught me that I am beyond what happened to me, and not only am I victorious, but I am also an overcomer. I am a very capable person who is able to live a healthy and happy life. I must choose and make choices that are healthy, happy, and successful. Plus, the largest insight for me has been that I, too, deserve all of that: being healthy, happy, and successful. Thank you for reminding me again. I will pass along the information to Elizabeth Marie as well."

"Come and see me, Connie Jo, and we will go shopping down by the beach, and I'll make you your waffles, bacon, and eggs that you love so much."

"Really, Marisa, you spoil me so much! How lucky am I to know such a beautiful person as yourself, and to call you my friend and sister. I am so honored and grateful to be blessed by you and your love! Alright, count me in. As soon as June gets here, we can meet up and celebrate our birthdays together because we are both summer babies! Please check your work calendar, and I will check with my boss."

"Alright, baby girl. Call me day or night and remember, no one has one right way or a secret blueprint of living life, so read the Bible and take away the pieces that help you through your daily living."

I took a very long bath with bubbles and mango salt scrubs and just contemplated everything. I cried because I could not ease all the pain that Elizabeth Marie suffered, and I cried for myself. I know I am blessed to be able to move forward and have such an intelligent sister friend like Marisa, who is willing to share her knowledge and life experiences with me so that I can grow as a person. I also know that it is my Lord who carries me through and is teaching me to live my life fully. I am amazed at the people He has placed in my path to teach me the failed gaps of early childhood development I should have been exposed to and just wasn't. I am sure we all have something we are going through, and we each walk the path of discovering self-help tools to better our lives.

I drained the water and refilled the tub, this time turning on music and singing at the top of my lungs I was just enjoying the moment of good smells and relaxation. I knew I was going to sleep deeply and well tonight. Facing one demon at a time, I have learned it takes courage, and it can hurt profoundly, but when you come out on the other side, oh, how sweet and peaceful it is.

Chapter 6

Romando

Out of all Mami's children, it was the youngest child who was the toughest to locate. At the going away picnic given so that all siblings, foster care, and adopted families had the opportunity to mingle and interact one final time prior to adoption, Mami's youngest son was Romando. He was only three when he went to be with his new family. Almost all his infant and toddler stages of developmental milestones had been learned during the time that he spent in foster care. Every week of visitation that was among the siblings was the only time he was able to connect and establish a relationship with the rest of us. Truth be known, he was more into his foster family than his biological family and could never understand why we couldn't all be together after the end of our visits.

His foster parents said he would bawl and punch his pillows, wanting his big brother and sisters with him, and did not understand why he couldn't see them anymore.

Romando had a different father than we girls did, but he was beloved by all. Tall for his age, he resembled his dad in every way. He was always moving, active early, and curious about his surroundings. He babbled early and was talking and laughing sooner than most his age. One of my last memories of Romando was when Mami had driven us to Auntie Luna's house and, when Auntie was not there, had left her a gift with the neighbors. While she was away dropping off the gift, the rest of us were in the car waiting, windows down, wiggling, dancing, and singing at the top of our lungs to "The Hustle" by Van McCoy. In the meantime, Romando crawled over the back seat, rolled down the driver's side window the rest of the way, honked the horn, and accidentally shifted the gear into drive. We went from singing to screaming for help as we saw Mami running her heart out to get to us; she was about one hundred feet away. Meanwhile, Mr. Garcia, our auntie's neighbor friend, had seen the turquoise 1956 Chevrolet Bel Air Coupe in motion—the minute it was put into gear—and was already jumping into the car, hitting the brakes. Mami got to the car and hugged every one of us, saying she was sorry she had even left the vehicle for a minute. She would never do that again. After we had all stopped crying, we ended up smiling again when Mami pulled out a box from the trunk full of our favorite red apples and some orange juice. Since we had had so much excitement, instead of going to the church carnival as planned, we ended up at the park down the street, playing on the swings and the merry-go-around. It is a great memory of my youngest brother and his curiosity getting the best of him. He was so adventurous even then.

One evening, our youngest sister, Sandrida, called and excitedly insisted I check a profile on social media because her children, the twins, had located someone she believed was our youngest brother, but she was not sure if she had the last name spelled correctly. Romando Mostasa was his adopted name, and according to social media, he was in Arizona.

"Constance, our brother only lives a few hours away from us. Can you believe it? I know there is a huge chance that it may not be him, but I am just sure in my heart that it is our little brother, I just know it!"

I had looked him up while we were on the phone and verified that he looked exactly like his dad and even appeared tall and thin like his father. Thrilled to know that she was right, Sandrida said they were calling him right away and to pray he would be willing to speak with them. She would call back in a day or two if they were successful. Before getting off the phone, I mentioned to Sandrida that Mami had a message for him because he truly had a mental condition and struggled with his emotions and prescribed drugs, and at times, street drugs, and for her to be cautious because he may be in a half-way home or going through some personal issues we are not aware of. If he is on medication, for example, he might not be as responsive and enthusiastic as she is to find him.

"Oh, Constance, do you believe everything Mami said to you was true? But, alright, I will just reach out and see if it is him. I promise I won't move him into my house on the first weekend."

Two days later, Sandrida called me back and was so surprised that I was at the airport waiting for her to come and pick me up. She laughed, and shared she was on her way, and our brother is moving in and will stay with her for a while because he is struggling in his current city and needs a fresh start. He did not want to be in the car again, after riding to Sandrida's house from his place, about four hours away. It was the longest road trip he had taken in a while, but he was waiting to speak with Constance at her house.

Sandrida shared that Romando did not remember a lot from our past, but he was able to name all his brothers and sisters and even recalled a few Austin, Texas memories. One of his most vivid recollections was the infamous Zilker Metropolitan Park we used to go to as children for our sibling and family child protection visitation meetings when the weather was nice. He remembered seeing a beautiful lady that would hold him on her lap and ride the park train throughout the botanical garden areas. He could also vaguely recall the huge natural spring hole they called the swimming pool at the same park.

Those were wonderful times. We took photos, ate snacks, and laughed a lot.

Standing at six feet three inches, Romando was the spitting image of what I remembered of his dad. He walked toward me and said, "I know you are Constance, my sister. I have been going through photo albums with Sandrida and have seen a bunch of photos of you through the years."

After enjoying a comfortable conversation about his and my adopted family, I had asked him if he was interested in a message that Mami had left for him because she knew one day we would find him, but she would be long gone.

He had looked at me with a lifted eyebrow and said, "Sure, I want to know anything that my birth mom would want me to know, especially if it is about me or my birth dad."

So, quoting Mami, I began. "'Baby boy of mine, a love child wanted and adored, you are quiet, witty, and so handsome like your father. He was a good man, and when you are ready, please come to Austin and search for him; he will still be in the Austin area. Back in the day, he was so determined to move all of us to Mexico, where he came from, that I had to leave him because I would never agree to move the family away from my family origins and had no desire to begin a new life in a different country when everything that meant anything to me and loved beyond my own life was right here in the heart of Texas! What better place to be than the capital of Texas, our beloved Austin, Texas?

"'Child, the one thing you must address and know about is your mental health challenges because you suffer what I have, and it requires your full attention. Remember to eat healthily, fill your plate with vegetables, lentils, and proteins such as a variety of white cheeses and meats. Stay away from processed foods or anything that comes in a box. Remember, instead of craving candy, choose fruits, and if you must, make cakes and candy from scratch so you can choose healthier ingredients. You won't have the desire to sleep for long periods of time, but you must learn ways to relax and rest. Turn off your mind in a way that you seek peace and tranquility. Silencing the mind with meditation is a good way to do this. Choose to exercise and move for at least thirty minutes a day, and most importantly, seek a group or a place to pray or find a support group that grows your mind and heart.

Romando Josefino, since you will love being outdoors, choose an active sport that does not cost much and is safe.

"'When you seek a mentally soothing activity, choose something to teach you there is something beyond yourself to lean and rely on for guidance. Your restless emotional struggles are real, and son, the medications they have you on do work if you will take them on a regular basis and continue to work your plan for success. Do not be ashamed to have a support group of assisted living to make it through life because your condition is real and requires help from others on occasion. If you do not follow my words, then you are doomed to turn to street drugs, and your drug of choice will end you up with legal issues and struggles you do not want to be a part of. Please focus on staying healthy, and I am so sorry that by the time this message gets to you, you will have lost a child and struggled through many relationships. You have the will to thrive, and you will make it through this life, but don't be embarrassed that it will require a support system to instruct and cheer you on every step of the way. Baby boy, you will always be my baby, and I love you and am so proud of the person that you have become. You are special because you are Romando Josefino. You have talents and skills that allow you to succeed, but you must be willing to do the work and always turn to the spiritual for direction and to find your peace. You have a good heart and such a genuine desire to do right. Seek that path, and you will find joy in this lifetime. Never forget you are loved and have always been wanted.'"

Romando simply got up from where he was sitting and hugged me tight, his eyes misty. "You don't know how much I needed to hear that. How did she know what I am going through now and that I ended up with a mental illness requiring medication to survive daily? Plus, it is true. I end up at an assisted living home just to find support to make sure I take my medication, eat right, and remember to incorporate routines and nutrition daily. If it weren't for my half-way home family, I'd be on the streets making poor choices. It is important for me to go to my support groups, and I also choose to go to church weekly so that I will have some sort of social connection to the real world."

"Romando, do you have any questions? What are your thoughts on us finding you?"

"Well, I just want to have some photos of my mother and dad and of my siblings. I want to know where you all live now, and I am hoping to go to Austin one day and desire someone who can help me locate my dad. I am also anticipating that someone will show me our old neighborhood, just so that I have something about my origins to imprint in my mind as the original place that I came from. I vaguely remember the pretty lady that used to hold me on the train at a park or would hold my hand as we walked through a park, and it would seem more real to me if I could go there and be where I used to be versus it just seeming like something I made up, like a movie I keep repeating in my dreams. Finally, if, by some miracle, my real dad is alive, I would like to meet him."

"When you are ready, you just let me know, and I will meet you in Austin. We can stay with our brother or auntie. By the time you are ready to visit, so much of East Austin will have changed, but I can be like a tour guide and show you what used to be and how things were when we were little. I love you, little brother, and am so grateful you have been found. Wherever you are at, you can call me anytime, and when I visit Arizona, I do hope to visit you as well."

Through the years, Romando calls me, and I send him boxes by mail to surprise him wherever he is living. He speaks of his love for his adopted parents, especially his mother, who has not ever wavered in helping him when he has struggled through life. He is proud to be loved by her, especially since he has not been able to reconnect with this birth mom like he had hoped to, but is so excited to have so many more siblings. He knows he is not alone in the world.

Chapter 7

San Antonio

Constance had surrounded herself with her favorite sandy shoreline items as she sat on a low beach chair at her favorite Gulf of Mexico beachfront near Galveston, Texas, right before one takes the ferry ride to cross over to Galveston Island. Her seashore was called Emerald Beach and had some of the quaintest coastline bungalows in the area. Mostly because of the maximum mesmerizing tranquil sunsets, filled with glorious deep colors of oranges and golden yellows against the distant aqua horizon. Constance had a historical special hideaway that few people knew about, and if you happened to know about it, it was truly a treasure to explore. It was just five minutes from her beach, hidden in plain sight. It was called Fort Travis Seashore Park and was located right before the ferry landing. This treasure was built in 1816 during an expedition for Spain and used to protect explorers from the Karankawa Indians.

Marisa owned a cottage nearby and had allowed Contance to get away and just vacation there by herself one weekend before school began. Constance, at the time, was a social worker at one of the elementary schools in Beaumont, Texas, and just wanted to meditate and make some calls to her siblings. Today, she was returning Elizabeth Marie's call and request to chat about San Antonio and the medicine men she had never heard of or known about.

Sitting on the low fuchsia beach chair, Constance had created an office with a table, notebooks, and memo pads she was using as her personal diaries. She also had pencils, markers, and pens to write with and take notes from her conversations with her siblings. She had located a huge umbrella and had angled it so that the sun was not in her face. After making some sun tea with freshly squeezed mandarin oranges and a fresh batch of fruit cocktail with coconut shavings and pecans, she was ready to call her sister.

Answering the phone, Elizabeth Marie giggled as she stated she had a feeling today would be our lengthy conversation for her to learn about the San Antonio visits.

"Honestly, Elizabeth Marie, don't you ever just want to live life right now and leave everything else as it comes?"

"No sister. My way of knowing works for me because I know that my life is short, so I must pack in every activity and adventure I wish to experience before my life is cut short—if not today. Let me tell you about my personal life, the man that I recently met, and when we are getting married. He is the one who will take the time to love me, protect me, and be a part of my life. He will be the longest relationship that I have, but I know my happiness will be but a few years. I know, sister, you don't want to know the details, but I will call back again so we can discuss because he will be the father of my only child, your niece."

"Oh my gosh, Elizabeth Marie, if you would rather cover this very important topic versus my visits to the medicine men with Magdelina, by all means, let's do that."

"No, no, because I have my notebook ready to take notes and have been looking forward to listening about the voodoo men from San Antonio."

Laughing, Constance began. "Alright, but you don't get out of telling me details about my future niece just because you want to learn about the mystical world of our family and especially those closet skeletons!

"So, you see, the first time that I remember going to see our grandmother's two distant relatives named Victorio and Geronimo, Magdelina and I were incredibly young. I don't even know why we were the ones chosen to go with her. I had just turned four, and she was going to turn six the following month. Grandmother told us they were the medicine men, shamans, voodoo healers, or curanderos, but we were to know they were relatives, connected through the roots of her momma, our great-grandmother. We could call them 'tios,' which means uncles in Spanish, or 'primos,' which means cousins. She did not want us to fear these men, so right before we got to their place in San Antonio, she would begin singing a song, 'Cu, ru, ru, ru....cu, ru ru ru.' This would start at least ten minutes before we arrived at our destination. Then she would be knocking on our primo's door. "Cu, ru, ru, ru...cu, ru, ru, ru, here comes Victorio, here comes Geronimo to say hello.'

"I can remember this song because she would also sing it to us to calm us down or hold us to make us go to sleep in our toddler years when she was being kind. I remember hearing these words in a dull, gentle, singsong manner."

"Oh, sister, now that you say this, I do remember 'cu, ru, ru, ru,' but not the other words."

"What was odd was our grandmother had a car, but she never drove a day in her life. Instead, she would have one of our uncles or great-uncles drive her to San Antonio. The other thing that always seemed odd to me and Magdelina was that we would have to go to the farmer's market until the sun went down, then in the dark, we would make our way to this same old raggedy house. I have no clue about the address or where it is located. Don't even recall anything nearby, except that we were downtown at the farmer's market until it got dark, and then we'd be driving what seemed to be in circles for a long time before the car would stop, and grandmother would tell us to be very quiet and just to follow her.

"Since we were children, all I clearly remember are the many colors of the house, like pink, sage, white, and light blue. Almost like they started painting the house and then decided they did not like the color, so they were trying a different color on a different section of the house. The home appeared unkept, and the porch needed repairs, with many rotting steps on the staircase ascending to the top of the porch. To make it worse, some of the windows were broken, and a few windows were completely missing but were covered with cardboard. There were pink metal flamingos scattered throughout the house border as decorations, and within what appeared to be a garden patch against the far-right corner of the front end of the house was a maze big enough for anyone to get lost in. There were also porch and landscape lights throughout the pathway leading to the front steps, but instead of the usual white lights, they were red and green. Not sure if this meant anything, but they were dim, making it appear haunted and spooky to us as children. I recall our grandmother walking up to the door, and instead of ringing a doorbell or knocking, she would call out the 'cu, ru, ru, ru' song, then wait ten seconds, then call out again, 'cu, ru, ru, ru.'

"Out of nowhere, the door would pop open, and she would enter, telling us to stay very close to her. Our uncles, her sons or great uncles, her brothers, who drove us to this place, rarely went inside; instead, they would tell her they would pick her up in a couple of hours and leave. Most of the time, it was usually Tio Vino and Tio Petro that took her.

"Thinking about this right now, I remember a couple of other odd things that struck me as unusual now that I am an adult. First, she would wear these flowing long outfits that were sheer and shiny with vibrant colors. We are talking hues of golds, oranges, lime greens, purples, reds, and just plain glittery. She always had her hair pinned up and pulled back out of her face, wrapped in thickly crocheted or knitted floppy headwear. Always a ball or tassels with color of some sort with jingling sounds like a bell. What stood out was that she was never able to control her wild curly hair, so you'd see strays of curls here and there. I can remember just thinking that *I have a pretty grandma*. Honestly, I don't even think the tops and bottoms that she wore even matched; they were just loud with bright colors. Before she entered the house, she would take a little bottle of oil—smelled like mint or lavender—and rub it over the tops of her hands, inside the palms of her hands, and on her forehead. On her forehead, she would make the sign of a cross. The other odd thing that happened on this night, and I don't even know why I remember this, was that she had documents showing to the medicine men that she had gotten 'insurance' on me and Magdelina. You know, I never thought of this until I went through documents that were given to me by Mami. As poor as our grandmother was, she always had insurance policies for all her children and grandchildren. I wouldn't think anything of this any other time, but when our uncle died in the car crash, I do recall how they called her a wise, rich woman and smart to have an insurance policy for him because it would cover the funeral and leave her with some extra money even though it would never bring him back. Still, as an adult, I always thought this was odd, but with her casting spells, do you think she anticipated that eventually we would all 'accidentally' die of something?" *I just wonder.*

Elizabeth Marie exclaimed, "Oh my goodness, sister, our own grandmother was plotting out our demise and gaining money from it? Shouldn't she have gone to jail for this?"

"So, what happened on this visit was she had her fortune read, and you could hear her screaming and telling the shaman curanderos to take it back and undo their cruel prophecy of the ending of her youngest child. Magdelina and I looked at each other with huge eyes, crying. We were scared because now they were having to hold our grandmother down because they told her no spell could ever reverse his destiny, so she needed to spend every waking moment with him until his time was up on this earth. It would be cut short and soon. On a stormy night, bound with love and his best friend, our uncle would vanish into the night, crashing into a pole that he would not see coming. Our grandmother's only comfort would be knowing later that his wife would have a child and he would reincarnate and carry his name's sake and likeness. After this visit, I do remember our grandmother casting spell after spell. She was like a mad woman driven to insanity, trying to find ways to reverse what was foretold to her that rainy, misty San Antonio visit to the medicine men's home.

"I would be almost six years old when our grandmother's youngest son would hydroplane into a light pole, transitioning into eternity beyond the living. That was the first time in my life I understood a person could say something out loud, and it would come true. In this case, the old shaman curanderos were right; it was the telling of the ending of a life near and dear to our grandmother. In my opinion, after the death of our uncle, she became meaner and hollower inside. She drank more and was more hateful and full of vengeance, not caring who she hurt, just that they were as miserable as she was. She was never the same after the death of her youngest baby boy. He was only eighteen when he died."

"Constance, I haven't even been asking my usual thousands of questions because this is all new to me, and I am flabbergasted to hear all of this firsthand for the very first time. Do you realize what this means? Our grandmother was truly a medicine woman, a shaman who really was paid to cast spells. Now all her little dolls with pins in them, her little bottles of ointments, animal hair and parts, like her chicken feet, people's pieces of fabric off their clothing, and herbs make total sense. I used to get in big trouble trying to eat her herbs, and she would yell that it was going to make me sick and I should not touch her bottles. I do remember their alcoholic concoctions that they would ferment and make into moonshine, usually any available fruit they grew in the orchard. I remember apples, peaches, cherries, pomegranates, lemons, and blackberries, plus they would add honeysuckle, grapefruit, boysenberries, and figs."

"Elizabeth Marie, isn't it bizarre what we remember? I also remember these same fruits being preserved for the winter and used for jams and jellies. See how we can have such good memories and, at the same time, such sad and painful ones. Why couldn't our family just have been a healthy one with successful relationships that weren't so toxic? Makes me sad thinking of what could have been."

"Constance, that is enough remembering the past for today. Thank you for sharing, and I am so grateful you and Magdelina are alive today to share your stories of your San Antonio visits. To me, it is fascinating and a little terrifying because I can't imagine exposing children to that environment so young. Also, you two should have been in bed resting for school instead of trolling the streets with a bunch of old creepy men learning about voodoo and enchantments. Hey, what the heck do I hear in the background screeching? Sounds like a bird."

"Yes, sister, it is a bird. A seagull, to be exact. I am at the beach just enjoying the waves, listening to our conversation, and being grateful knowing that our Lord gives us boundaries and even the winds and the seas obey him. That is why I love being where the ocean meets the sand or, in this case, the Gulf of Mexico meets the sand. The sea breeze is kissing my face with a light, cool wind. Very relaxing and calming. I think that I shall be here for another hour writing in my diary, then I will pack it up and take the ferry over to Galveston and eat at my favorite place called Fish Tales. Followed by a stroll down the strip to many of my favorite tourist trap shops.

Elizabeth Marie squeals. "Please eat a shrimp po'boy for me!"

"You already know that I will. Plus, I will splurge on my preferred shrimp kisses and brownie volcano for dessert! Just imagine shrimp kisses with smoked gouda, wrapped in bacon and grilled. Can't be healthy for me but still the best seafood ever invented along the shores of Galveston. Who can deny splurging on a hot caramel brownie with a scoop of vanilla bean Blue Bell ice cream, plus, hot fudge and whipped cream on the top? Uh, and don't forget the cherry on top! Death by Chocolate is just the way to go on a hot summer day! Just thinking about this makes my mouth water. So much for the health kick I was on. Okay, Elizabeth Marie, I shall get off the phone now and run up and down my Emerald Beach a few times before lunch. I will feel less guilty when I indulge in that dessert we just discussed.

"I love you, sister. Let me let you get off this phone, and the next time we talk we shall go over whatever comes to your mind and heart, alright?"

"I love you to the moon and back! Always and forever, you are my best friend, and I love you more than my own life. Constance, next time we speak, I want you to document my words to my unborn child. It is important to me, and I have a list for her to consider."

"Elizabeth Marie, you already know it is a girl?"

"Sister, please, of course Annabeth Marie is a girl! She is special and perfect in every way to me. I love her beyond anything unique in this universe. Constance, can you believe the Lord will grant me my wish in this lifetime? I am so blessed and grateful."

"Okay, Elizabeth Marie. Next time we will cover your daughter's letter that you will leave for her in my book. Bye for now."

Chapter 8

Sandrida

The youngest of the girls, Sandrida, was nonstop on the go from the minute she was born. Her giggles could be heard from down the neighborhood street because she truly was lighthearted and loved by anyone who met her. A thin frame and a petite child with prominent almond-shaped hazel eyes like Mami's, she looked as dainty as a porcelain doll with light brown hair and the longest black eyelashes. Enormous bouncing curls edging her stunning dainty face. The only thing that stood out was a lazy eye that had to be corrected with surgery. This was something Mami would not ever tend to, and through the years, we learned they called it medical neglect of basic health needs.

Later, Mami would explain that she did set up appointments to get the medical attention Sandrida needed, but when the time came, she usually was on one of her mental health breakdowns where nothing mattered except getting away. Over a period of missing scheduled appointments, the doctors would not even set up a meeting for care because Mami was not going to follow through, and they told her when the time was right, she would need to work with a social worker to ensure follow through with her daughter's needs. It would be critical that the surgery Sandrida required be addressed before Sandrida entered elementary school. It was serious that she was able to see correctly in a classroom environment. Sadly, even up to the time that Mami lost parental rights, this procedure was not ever addressed.

After a year of tears and begging, Elizabeth Marie had talked her adopted parents into legally adopting Sandrida and bringing her home to Arizona so that she would not have to be in foster care all her life. Constance spoke to Sandrida often over the phone and loved her dearly. She was usually more intense and emotional with her feelings and statements of the past. She would often share that even though she remembered stuff that happened to us because she was four when they took us away permanently, she honestly does not recall the worst of things like I or the older kids did. She mostly remembers certain houses and playing outside in the yard watching Papi, our dad, mow the lawn, but she can't even remember his face or anything significant about him other than he was our Papi. She does recall her godmother being a different person than the older children's godparents and going to many church functions, including carnivals and baptisms. As far as our relatives were concerned, she remembers our aunties and uncles, although probably will get their names mixed up because there were so many of them, especially up in Hill Country where the wild thistles grow.

There at Hill Country, in the middle of roaming hills, pecan trees, and orchards of fruits, were a substantial number of the family spending time together on the ranch eating and collecting fruits from the orchards and vegetables from the multiple gardens. They roast animals, smoke a variety of meats, create scrumptious dishes, even can foods to store in the family man-made underground cellar for the winter months. There were plenty of canned, smoked, cooked, and baked foods that the out-of-town relatives took bags full of. The children were often loaded up in the back of a couple of classic pick-up trucks and toted a mile to where a grove of pecan trees was at and given buckets to collect the nuts. One could hear laughter from the children as they ran from one end of the grove to the other chasing each other and gathering pecans. The older teens could be seen cracking and eating pecans and carving names into the trees. The aunts and uncles monitoring would bring out baskets of homemade breads, butter, and cheese and serve the bunch on picnic blankets. Freshly made lemonade and homemade pecan and apple pies were shared by all present. Those are wonderful memories Constance never wants to let go of from the past. Even now, the memory of soft winds bringing in the smells of honeysuckle and peaches is nostalgic. Those are the good times of Hill Country and have a place in the heart and soul when understanding why Mami would go back even though so much inappropriate activity occurred on the family property as well.

Snapping herself out of her head and back to the present, Constance is absorbing Sandrida's perception. Mostly, Sandrida remembers walking the streets of Austin, always looking for Mami, searching for her return. She also recalls digging for food at the grocery store dumpsters and spending a lot of time in the dark at night because the lights did not come on in the house.

As children, we had learned that it was lighter under the moon during the night hours, so we'd lug the bed mattress outside. We loved to sleep under the stars because we could see more clearly, and we felt safer under the moonlight. Looking into the heavens, we learned from our Hill Country family that the stars tell our destiny and guide us throughout our lives. Never once did we think that someone could possibly kidnap us from the yard. We were all under the age of eight, after all.

Even as a young child, Sandrida was stunning. Her face had perfect model-like features with those enormous eyes, complete with dreamy intelligent gazes. She was symmetrically perfect. Her face was framed with long strands of generous curls. What was striking about her was her tanned skin against those hazel eyes that were exactly the color of Mami's. It depended on what she wore as to what color they appeared to be. They could resemble blue, green, gray, light brown, or somewhere in between the ocean and the sea. Mesmerizing. Another feature that was just like Mami was her five feet six inches in height. If she wore size zero, I would be surprised. Scanning her, one would believe her so delicate that any gust of wind would blow her over. She walked like a princess: always head held high, eyes forward, with naturally graceful limbs. Such a beautiful girl indeed. One minute she would be docile and compliant, and the next thing you knew, she was an unleashed tyrant unpredictable on what got her upset. At school, they would have to work on self-regulation skills so that she could best interact with her classmates. Over the years, she grew into a lovely, modest young lady. Mind you, she always spoke her mind and made it clear she was not beyond defending herself if needed.

On one of the many trips that I took to Arizona as a young adult, I was able to give her Mami's message. "Sandrida, before Mami dies, she told me to pass on her message to you."

"Constance, what are you talking about? I talk to her over the phone, and she sounds terrific so don't speak of her death like it is actually going to happen anytime soon."

"Well, you will need to speak with her because before she dies, she says you will bring your twins and husband to visit her, and it will be one of the happiest days of her life to see her grandchildren, and she wants to thank you for that."

"Hey, wait up. She said I will have twins? Oh my gosh! When and what do I need to do to get ready? Constance, let me not lie to you. I just found out this past week I am going to have a boy and a girl. We did not want to tell everyone about being pregnant with twins until I felt comfortable that they were healthy and my pregnancy was going well. My gosh! How in the heck does she know details of my life? I want to know what else she knows. Also, we are not married."

"Sandrida, you may not be legally married, but you have been together long enough to be considered married, and you will be together a long, long time. Mami said your husband must learn to place his family first and he won't until the very end of his life. When his time is nearing exiting this world, then and only then will he understand how important his family is, and his time is best spent with those who have loved him and cared for him all along—not his chasing of greener pastures. "Honestly, Sandrida, your relationship hardships will have you leaving him, and you will end up staying with one of the twins.

"Mami states that you must find ways to be strong and be of good courage because it is important you value yourself. You are so precious and deserve the best that life gives you, but first you must learn to take care of yourself. Get a job and begin buying stuff for yourself besides the necessities. Take up a hobby, try something new, or save up money and go visit family in Texas. Even better, take a trip somewhere you have never been and try something new there. It will remind you of what a deserving individual you really are and help you to feel better about yourself. Sandrida, life will have many ups and downs for you, but working a job is your freedom. Do it for a while even though you prefer to stay at home and just be with family. Mami said to take up a pastime you enjoy, like coloring, music, making jewelry, sewing, cooking, whatever you choose. Try something unfamiliar; just do something that is for you only. Don't worry, your turn of goodness financially will come, but like me, it will come in your later years of life.

"One other thing Sandrida. As much as you do not like going to the doctor, make sure when you have stomach issues that you go. It will not be something to ignore because it can be serious to your health. Don't take it lightly when this area hurts. Remember that as her baby girl, Mami loves you dearly and is so sorry that her mental illness and demons of her past kept her from being the best mother she should have been to you. She is sorry she failed you when you needed your eye fixed. Please forgive her. She is also saddened that she was not physically there for you when you needed her as a toddler. You are truly a baby girl who could have benefited from extra hugs and one-on-one attention. This does not take away her love for you or her belief that you can do anything or be anything that you want to be. You are beautiful inside and out."

"Constance, those are the most beautiful words I have ever heard. Mami loved me, and even though she wasn't mentally healthy or even an involved parent, I do remember when she was there with us and for us. We would go grocery shopping with her, to the parks, church, picnics, and have parties in the backyard with a lot of people. I just wish I could remember her tucking me into bed at night, teaching me to ride a tricycle, or even taking us trick-or-treating on Halloween night. I only recall our Tia Luna doing that. It makes me sad because I remember when we were toddlers growing up, there were rarely moments of active parenting and safely living our daily lives. I will be the opposite of her. I plan to be there for my children, make sure they have what they need, and I won't miss a doctor's visit ever. You wait and see. My children will have nice clothes. They will eat well, and they will be clean and taken care of from morning until morning. No excuses. They will also go to family gatherings, church, and school regularly. Just wait. Life will be different for my babies and grandchildren. I will always put my family first. That is what I walked away with from my early childhood. My family matters, and I am the one who can choose to be there for them no matter what."

Sandrida is crying now, and we just hold each other. In lullaby tones, I whisper, "We can't take away what was, but we can control now and our world, our future, and we will. I love you, Sandrida. You are right. What happened to us in the beginning of life should have never been, but we are here now and can do better, and we shall. I am grateful that I took this vacation to be with you. I am so proud of you and so happy that we had this talk."

Chapter 9

Sister Bond

Prior to leaving Sandrida and Elizabeth Marie during a monsoon season visit, we had this amazing idea to call Magdelina and connect while we were together. We gathered two phones, one from the kitchen and one from the living room, and propped them up to a speaker, and we dialed Magdelina to see if she could tell who was speaking with her on the phone. We all burst into tears of laughter because no one could tell who was laughing and who was talking; we sounded so much alike. Magdelina insisted we call out who was speaking and then answer or ask questions. It was such an odd sensation for us to hear ourselves all together, just like when we were children.

Magdelina called out, "Does anyone remember taking out the mattress from the house to be in the backyard looking at the stars and then sleeping out there all night long?"

We laughed and all stated simultaneously, "Of course. Who could forget?"

Even as young toddlers, we would be placed on a mattress by the elders and allowed to sleep under the stars. We were taught that our destiny was written in the twinkling lights of the deep, dark skies. Even the wise men looking for our Savior in the Bible followed the star to our newborn king. Each depth of the winding galaxy path had tales and destinations for each of us, and if we learned the secrets of the moon and constellations, we would have our whole lives foretold before us. All we had to do was listen to the elders, practice their secrets and spells, and search for the spirits that rule the universe. Always seek knowledge or wisdom and only spread goodness and truth. Each of us, in our own way, would learn that we had gifts and could use them to better this world.

Contance had to know. "Who remembers going to the park by the river?"

Everyone yelled out, "Me!"

We giggled as Elizabeth Marie shared. "My favorite part of going to the park was when Mami gave us Cheetos and grape juice, and we were allowed to play on the swings. It was so much fun swinging to the sky and being together."

Sandrida declared, "Now that I think about it, I do remember sitting in the middle of the merry-go-round and getting dizzy, but it was fun."

Then Magdelina excitedly said that she loved going to the swimming pool and just being at the low end in the water on a hot summer day.

As we giggled and reminisced about days long gone, it was Elizabeth Marie who asked the next question. "When did you realize that we had a brother besides Romando?"

Magdelina shared. "I always knew about Francisco because when we were little, we would go to Hill Country, and we were told, "Here is your brother Francisco. He lives here on the ranch with some of your cousins, but he is your real brother and loves you. Take time to get to know him and play with him while you are visiting." Magdelina continued. "We'd spend days just playing throughout the ranch, then someone would load us up on the back of a pickup truck, and we'd end up in the orchards collecting fruits and pecans to bring back to the adults for baking and cooking."

Constance added, "Me too. It's like I always knew Francisco was our brother. I just couldn't understand why he couldn't be with us all the time. I remember him being quiet and shy, but he had such a beautiful smile. You know, when I first started visiting Mami in Austin, she immediately told me to stop by and visit my brother because he was living in Waco, Texas, with one of our cousins, and it was on the way to Austin. So, I did. I was nineteen, and Francisco was twenty-five. He had a girlfriend and was easy to speak with. He enjoyed taking us out to eat. He especially loved music and dancing. He was always a person of little words and was observant and appeared content. I just remember thinking; this is my brother, and I love him."

Our phone call had to come to an end because Elizabeth Marie and Sandrida's mom came into the living room where we were on the floor listening intently around the phones and told us to get off the phone. "Who is going to pay for the long-distance phone call that was now going on ten minutes long?" Honestly, she couldn't understand why we were all together yet had to be on the phone.

Through the years, we would spend time here and there connecting as sisters and mostly wanting to know what we were doing and where we were in life. Going to school, college, being in the military, getting married, having babies and so much more. There was not a time that we connected that we did not feel a deep and special sister bond. We wondered if going through some of the things that we did at such a young age made us closer. We knew we had each other forever, for the rest of our lives, if we chose to stay in touch with one another. It was a great sister bond and a special kind of love.

Chapter 10

Francisco

As long as I can remember, there has always been an understanding that we had an older brother and there were reasons why he was being raised by other members of the family. Also, we have known all our lives the reason that he was raised by our great-grandmother and great-uncles in Hill Country on the ranch had to do with the hate that my birth father had toward him. We heard rumors, but as children, we were never told the details until we reconnected with Mami as young adults.

Rumors in the family circles were that Francisco was a loving and good boy. When he was still in diapers, Mami supposedly made a tough decision to have him stay at the ranch. Constance later learned that Papi attempted to smother Francisco in between two mattresses when he was just three years old. When he was younger, still in diapers, he would not allow Mami to change his diapers, and he would get rashes, and worse, there would be maggots in the creases of his legs. The elders ran Papi off the ranch, and they chose to raise him on the ranch in Hill Country. Mami agreed he was safest away from her husband, who did not care for boys, and he had his reasons. All we knew was that Francisco was never adopted because he was never one of the children removed from the care of Mami any time that they placed us in foster care because he was always up at Hill Country. Therefore, she never had her rights taken away when it came to Francisco.

When Francisco turned fourteen, he went to live with a cousin and started working at the local H-E-B grocery store, returning carts to their spaces and bagging groceries. He completed high school, saved up, and bought his first motorcycle, and by the age of seventeen, worked and lived on his own. Well, he roomed with cousins near his age and split the bills. He was responsible and appeared older for his age.

Constance remembers on one of the trips to Austin, she had stopped in Waco, Texas, to visit Francisco, and he had introduced her to his sweetheart at the time. It was fun to meet the granddaughter of Conway Twitty, the country singer. Francisco used to say she was just a girl he knew in his younger years. On another visit, Constance met his fiancée and was sure that she had seen this girl in the past and started quizzing her. It was concluded that the reason she was familiar was because Lydia, Francisco's fiancée, had been married to Constance's godparents' middle son, and Constance had seen her visiting her godparents on a regular basis. Small world, but over time, Francisco and Lydia got married and lived in Austin.

Throughout the years, Francisco and Constance have seen one another and spent time together. The only message that Mami had for him, and we discussed it, was, "Francisco, my oldest child and beautiful son. Please forgive me for being the horrible person that I was back then and know that it was not your fault. It was never your fault. You were but an innocent, gorgeous baby boy. When I was raped, drugged, and left to die at the age of fifteen, all I could do was try to survive and escape my abuser. But I never truly escaped because I was pregnant with you. My dad believed that my abuser, your biological father, should make me an honest woman, so I was forced to marry him. We lived together for a year, but it did not work out because he chose to continue his bad habits of dealing, and I just hated him for ruining my life. We fought so much that, in the end, we divorced. When you were born, I just couldn't stand being around you because all I could think of was the abuse your dad inflicted on me. He was three years older than me, and in the beginning, we had so much fun riding motorcycles and fast cars. It was too late when I found out about how he made his money, and his temper at the time was due to drugs and lack of control. It was not fair how I made you pay for his bad treatment of me. Francisco, I pushed you away and refused to love you, and all you ever wanted was my love. I am saddened that you ever had to be rejected because of what I went through. Nothing on this earth can ever undo the pain I have caused you, and I deserve the hate and resentment you may have toward me. There are not enough words to say how much I regret my behavior and negligence."

Through the years, it was Francisco's father's sisters and our great-grandmother, great-aunts, and great-uncles who raised him, but it should have been his own mother. Mami needed so much help at the time with her own childhood trauma. It was not something she was familiar with; not until she was first institutionalized did she realize all the mental issues she had from her own sexual, physical, and mental abuse she endured through her childhood and older years. There aren't any excuses to make up, so she never did. Mami just apologized through the years, until her last breath. She would echo through the decades that Francisco deserved to have been loved and wanted by her and she was just so remorseful. There was a point Francisco chose to include her in his life, as an adult, and they did spend the latter part of her life devoting time together; getting to know one another.

Periods later, Francisco came to visit me in Beaumont, Texas, and he told me he had made peace with Mami. He had found religion that helped him to understand this world we live in belongs to Satan and his demons; sometimes, terrible things just happen to good people, and there is no other explanation other than it is Satan's domain. He realized Mami was a victim of abuse all her life, and she needed help. Francisco's dad had also found Jesus, and they had spent more time together now that Francisco was an adult. It is not like he was close to his dad, but they could at least be friends. Getting to know both his parents had been a process, and even though emotionally challenging, Francisco was glad he had invested in the time with each of them because he was emotionally in a better position to move on with his adult life and leave the pain of the past behind. Both of his parents had their own terrors to overcome, and Francisco was realizing it was their past challenges to overcome and not his. He was only responsible for himself and his own life.

One time in San Antonio, Francisco and Constance had taken Mami to meet up with Francisco's dad, who wanted to spend time with her. They had driven to Francisco's grandmother's home on his dad's side. When they drove up to a small white house with a white picket fence and beautiful tall old trees in the yard, Francisco's dad had been waiting for Mami and us to arrive. He stood there with a bouquet of flowers, a bottle of sparkling juice, and some glasses. Mami had been like a schoolgirl, laughing and smiling the whole time. Francisco Sr. kept staring at Constance and saying, "I just can't believe how much you look like your Mami when she was your age. It is unbelievable the likeness." It was a good conversation amongst all of them. He had asked Mami to marry him and to come and stay with him for the rest of her life. Mami declined his offer. She stated once again, "Francisco, I am so proud of your accomplishments and all that you have done to make your life a better one, but I can't leave my daddy's land, nor will I ever walk away from my Austin life, not even for an opportunity to be with you, once again. This time, it would be a good life, and for that I would be so grateful. My home is in Austin and in Hill Country. You are not willing to leave your home in Pasadena, and I am not willing to leave mine, but I do love you and will care for you the rest of my life." At that moment, Constance remembered seeing Francisco Sr. at the pink house, as he would periodically stop by and converse with Mami about his progress in life and ask her to come make a life with him as he had never remarried but always wanted to make things right with her, as she had been his love through the years. It was a bittersweet love story, and Constance witnessed on that day their love for one another. So sweet and tender.

For you see, since he had been getting his life together for years and was doing great for himself financially with a decent job, he had offered Mami to make it right. He wanted to remarry her and give her a nice home in Pasadena, Texas. Mami refused him every time because she would not leave her dad's land in Austin, Texas. Plus, she was happy that Francisco Sr. had found religion and was helping other people get off drugs, but she had her own life in Austin, and she was happy with it. She did encourage him and Francisco to continue to spend time together, but as for her, she had her own daily routines in Austin, and she was content also. To this day, Constance has one photo of them together from that visit, and one can clearly see their happiness together.

Sadly, it was reported that Francisco Sr. had been assisting someone get off drugs, and on one stormy night, they had come pounding on his door on an emergency assistance request. Francisco Sr. had bent over to unlock the door when shots were fired at the doorknob. The person he had been trying to help had come and stolen some valuable items and left him there to bleed to death. In the end, it was such a sad time for the family to absorb what happened, but others would simply say that karma gave him his fate for what he had done to Mami back in their teenage years. Francisco Jr. was grieving and sorrowful to finally build a relationship with his dad, only to lose him to death so soon.

Overall, Francisco made his peace and moved on with his life. He is a good older brother. Periodically, we make time to visit each other and call each other often. With social media, we attempt to connect and keep one another posted on our lives. We both enjoy motorcycle rides and appreciate our spiritual walk with our Lord, who sustains us through our trials and daily living. We each have a love for our Texas BBQ and try to attend Mami's maternal side family reunions even though they are far and few between. Francisco used to wonder if his life would have been better financially had he been adopted, but he is grateful he was not adopted because he is so close to our Mami's Hill Country, side of the family. All the bad incest and abusive ways from the old times are gone, and today, it is a safe and good place to visit and delight in family. There are very few acres of land that remain in the family name compared to back in the old days, but it is still a wonderful place to visit and enjoy its beauty and memories.

Chapter 11

Sunshine Letter

It was the beginning of November. Watching the last of the gorgeous foliage depart from the trees outdoors, Constance was getting ready for a cold winter. Hearing the phone ring, she knew it was Elizabeth Marie wanting to discuss her teardrop and sunshine letter to her daughter.

"Constance, I am so glad you picked up the phone. I couldn't wait to let you know that I am in love, and I just found out that we are pregnant, so we need to begin this letter to your niece, my daughter."

"Alright, sister. First, I love you, and I am glad that you called. Tell me, when did you get married, and how did you meet the father of your child, my niece?"

"I should have known you felt something. No one has told you that I got married."

"That's right, Elizabeth Marie. I just sense happiness and a homey family, which leads me to believe you as happy, married, and probably pregnant."

"It's my hometown in Arizona, and around here, that is the same as 'open USA border' filled with new husbands daily because they come in droves, and no one stops them from entering America. They seem to have more rights than what we do, those who are already citizens of our blessed country. I don't mind trying to help a good man who comes to the church seeking assistance and often marriage. Leonardo de Llano is a man who works and wants to provide for a family. He is in the construction business and is gone part of the year. We met at church at the food bank. He was volunteering. He gets assistance, but he wouldn't take it unless he could volunteer because, as he told the priest, he will not be in the same position—needing assistance—in a year from now because he plans to be self-sufficient by then. That was attractive to me, and even though others thought he was plain-looking, to me, he is handsome. Short and perfectly built. I really like his kind eyes and calm voice. He laughs a lot and gets my jokes. He also wants a child and wants to be married in America. Anyway, we have been married for five months now, and he lives with me and my parents. My parents like him and that is important to me too."

"Congratulations, and I hope that you are loved, valued, and happy. Are you ready to write your letter to your unborn child?"

"Thank you, sister, for loving me and just going with the flow. Please write this down and be open minded. Tell Annabeth Marie, beautiful daughter, you are wanted and loved beyond this world. Mami and Papi adore you, from your creation to your very last breath. You will be full of life and enjoy life for a very long time. Choose to live for you and for me. Every day, beautiful sweetness, my baby girl, reach for the moon in everything that you do. Go big or go home, never just halfway do a job, try a new hobby, or learn something new. Instead, learn every aspect of that hobby and search to acquire new skills. Give it all that you got and enjoy the little things of each detail in whatever you are learning. Live in the moment and enjoy just being you right now. Sit and look around you and tell yourself this is my life now, and I am grateful. I will never tell you a script to follow for your life, except fear is not of God, and making wise choices begins with having a spiritual relationship with our Lord, our Creator. We never understand everything that happens in our lives, but He provides us with people and opportunities to be successful, so Annabeth Marie, never quit and always offer thanks. Take that back. If you quit something, quit because it is not a healthy choice for you, or you have tried it and decide you prefer something better for yourself. It is alright, too, to change your mind. For example, if you are dating someone who may have personal issues which make your relationship toxic, baby girl, don't hesitate to run from that. Or, you are crazy about them, but they reject you for someone else, just think, 'man's rejection is God's protection' and move forward to something better. It is alright to move on with life toward a better tomorrow! You, Annabeth Marie, are loved and wanted, always."

Constance gazed at her sister's photo near the phone and sighed. "Elizabeth Marie, those are the most beautiful words. Makes me wish I was having a child so I could share my loving thoughts too."

"Sister, I don't want to give my child a must-do to-do list, but I want her to make choices that will set her up for the best that life has to offer, and this is why I am telling you now." There was a long pause on the line. "Even though my marriage will fail, not because of not loving this man but because he will want to return and live in his country, and I will want to be in my country where my child has the best educational opportunities and therapies that she will need. I know you don't understand all of this now, but it will make sense one day. Know this and remember it is my will that I want my child to be adopted by a family who will love her and challenge her to be her very best. She will be given chances and perceptions that she wouldn't have by not being adopted. I also have asked that she will live in or around our city in Arizona so she may always be near her birth family as well. She needs to be exposed to that part of her family, also. Finally, the list I wish for her to do is simple:

1. Love herself with the eyes of our Lord; love her family.
2. Work hard and stick to a career she finds rewarding.
3. Take up some hobbies that stretch her imagination.
4. Get as much education as possible.
5. Learn to enjoy cuisine in a way that she is interested in; exploring new tastes of different cultures.

6. Take up a sport that allows her to remain healthy.
7. Read books, watch movies, and enjoy music, plays, and novellas to her heart's content, and
8. Make sure she learns to drive safely.

Let her know that I am with her always, and she will know when it is me. My love for her is in her and all around her. To be absent from the body is to be present with our Lord, and our Lord is everywhere, therefore, I, too, am everywhere. When the wind is blowing, let it be my arms around her. When she smells salsa and tacos, she may know and desire her culture. When she showers and smells of freshness, may it be my tears of pride and joy for her being Annabeth Marie. When she searches for the moon and the stars at night, may she know her dreams can come true, and hope is endless. When she hears birds and sees the colorful butterflies around her, she will know that I am whispering 'I love you' and blowing kisses all around. May she never forget how valuable and treasured she truly is."

Constance had tears streaming down her face, and she knew then that Elizabeth Marie would get her request; the Lord would allow her to take Constance's fate of bearing a child and that of an early death. Constance's most favorite person in the world would be taken from her, and it would be final. Elizabeth Marie was crying also. "Please, sister, understand my depth of love for you is beyond the many universes we can't see, and I would give my life for you over and over. Please see to it that you finish our stories and complete your destiny so that your life may be restored and put back on track as it should have been. Also, know that it is okay. I am at peace with what will be."

All that Constance could do at that moment was cry and love her little sister. "Elizabeth Marie, you will have some of the best times of your life, filled with more joy than anything you have ever experienced because of this gorgeous little girl. Make every day a success by just taking in each moment with intentional activity and time well spent together. I love you."

Elizabeth Marie bellowed, "I am already so happy with my husband, and preparing for this baby is going so great, and it is such a wonderful time in our home. Even though I have had a few minor medical issues, that is nothing to the joy of being pregnant. I can feel her growing and developing in my tummy, and it is an experience I will never forget to be comforted and grateful for. I am in awe that I get to fill my days with having a creation in my body that will walk this earth and do terrific things that will be perfect for her life. She will grow up to be such an incredible person. Such a normal girl without all the tragedy and suffering we endured as children. She will only know goodness. I know losing me will be tough on her, but the fact that I was granted her is my one thing in life I desired so desperately and is truly a treasure that only our God could provide, and He did that for me. Sister, make Annabeth Marie understand. I was not ever supposed to have any children, and the fact that it was granted, I then was not ever supposed to live to see her grow up from infancy to being a toddler, a preschooler, or even a preteen. I was supposed to have died at childbirth, and that was it, but a miracle happened, and I got to experience some of her developmental years, and that is a marvelous present from our Lord. I just can't express how grateful I truly am. Also, my beautiful sister, I will call you weekly with updates of everything about her so that you may experience having a baby too."

Constance is gasping for air, engulfed in her own sorrow yet happiness for her beloved sister. "Sister, I know, like Mami, you can tell the truth about the future, but I sure don't like it and wonder why any life must be taken before we grow old together. You and I, we have been through so much together, and you are the one person I have asked the God of this Universe to allow in my life for the rest of my life, and yet, He will choose to snatch you out of my world, I am in so much pain knowing you will expire before I consider it your time that I just can't function. To be alone in the world without our chats and time spent together, I just refuse to accept and hate it so much. I want to go instead of you so that you may live. How is life fair, and how does our Lord justify that as goodness? Honestly, if He is all powerful then He could just make another adjustment and allow you to continue life until you are a hundred. We have family that live older than that!"

"Constance, my sweet, lovely sister, you already know the answer to that. The truth be known, all the abuse we endured as children, I just can't get past mine like you have been able to because, even with therapy, I can't seem to shut it down in my mind; even when I sleep, I am haunted. It has been tough on my heart, body, nervous system, and unfortunately, will have taken a toll and wear my body out before it's time. Constance, I pray the psychological world can find a way to help children who suffer as I have so they may live longer than me because it is a tragic reality. People need to know if we can't deal with the past in healthy ways, mentally, it is our bodies that suffer healthwise and can, in the end, send you to an early grave. This is why I tell you to choose to embrace me in ways other than grief so that you will have a long life and live it for both of us. Please, my true love in my life, my joy, and laughter. Constance, please choose not to drown yourself in grieving for me because we will see each other again, and it will be a joyful eternal life, as it should have been the first time. Please know that the life after this one is real and endless. Our early lives are but vapors anyway. I love you. Let's go ahead and end this conversation today, and you can analyze like you do while I internalize each moment and word you have shared with me. We can talk again soon. For now, I am happily married, and my belly is growing with your niece. I am beyond thrilled, and in this moment, my purpose in life is being fulfilled. I live in bliss."

"Alright, baby girl, enjoy your blissful life and savor each moment. I truly must admit, this is the happiest I have ever heard you be, and I just love it! I better receive a photo of you and your bliss soon. We will speak with each other soon. I love you, too. Talk later, my loving baby sister."

With that, our conversation was over, and Constance was numb, yet happy, for Elizabeth Marie, wondering how many other families have members that sense the future and are accurate in their predictions. Surely, this is not normal. Isn't it odd, and wouldn't the population at large find it strange, our conversations we have about the past, heaven, and the future? Constance had to give her mind some rest and chose to play dance music, dance, and clean the house for the rest of the day. She showered and then cried herself to sleep, knowing everything Elizabeth shared would come true.

Chapter 12

Come Back

Elizabeth Marie called me one Saturday morning and asked me if I were sitting down because the time had come for her to tell me about the time that she had died for fifteen minutes and came back. She wanted me to know because she had been thinking of it and decided that since she already knew she would not be around by the time our stories were published, she wanted to share her version of the story so that I could give the information to her child when the time was right. Choking down the chocolate twist donut that I had treated myself to for staying away from sugar all week, I literally almost lost it.

"Elizabeth Marie, what in the heck fire are you talking about? This is not funny if you are just trying to scare me with one of your dramatic jokes just to get me all stirred up! Death is not something that you play with, so you better be straight with me, if you are going to discuss a serious topic. What brought this on? Did you go to church and get convicted?"

Laughing. "As your baby sister, I am here to say that I am not joking, and I am ready to converse with you about this, so get your cup of warm tea with mandarin squeezed oranges in it ready and call me back."

Click, the phone went silent. Constance looked over to the microwave just in time to hear the ding that it was hot and ready for her, complete with mandarin oranges in it. *How in the world did she even know I have tea being warmed up?* Constance wasn't hungry anymore, so she set her donut back in the small Shipley's box that it had come in and hurried to her bed, where she had propped her three pillows up and gotten herself in a cozy position as if to watch a movie, but instead reached for the phone ready to talk.

After three rings, Elizabeth Marie picked up the phone as Constance burst out, "Talk to me and tell me everything, even the color of the clothes you are wearing."

Constance hears a robust roar of laughter, and Elizabeth Marie's melodic voice begins. "Constance, remember years ago when my baby was born, and I told you everything went well?"

"Yes, minor complications, but you worked through them."

"Well, that was sort of true, but there is more to tell."

"This is what I hate about all of us: we wait until everything is good before we tell what challenges we have gone through. If people knew, maybe we would have more support, but no, we choose to struggle alone. Do you ever think that maybe that has something to do with our past?"

"Listen, Constance. Focus on the current topic at hand. It was getting close for my baby to be born, but I was having issues. I am going to leave the paperwork for you to have because it is all in the notes. Imagine the hospital setting; everything appears white except for the instruments they use for surgery. I was doing well for the most part, then out of the blue, my blood pressure sky-rocketed out of control, and the next thing I remember was I was looking at them taking my child out of my belly with a tong-like instrument, and it was lightning quick. Then, something was not right about my baby's health. Anyway, before that happened let me tell you that I was in this unbelievably gorgeous place. It was brighter than the sun yet cozy as a tree house in a garden of overflowing flowers. Everywhere you looked, nothing but more plants and flowers, amply more vivid than anything I have ever seen before, and oh, the smells, they were so pure and pleasing to the senses. Think of your most favorite smell, then, multiply by one hundred times the intensity—that was the deep, concentrated aroma that lingered. Made me want to leap for joy, but I was more concerned about my baby, so kept praying to be able to see and touch my little girl. Coming toward me, I instantly knew was the angel of death, asking me if I was ready to stay or if I wanted to try a little longer?

"I looked at death and said, 'How can you ask me such a question when you know I will choose my baby, Annabeth Marie, every time? I have wanted a child for so long that I was willing to suffer abuse from my first husband just to get to my second husband, who loves me. My love for my baby girl is deeper than the multiple universes that exist, and my endless desire to be with her and see her grow up into a lovely woman, having her own wonderful family and life, is what pushes me to want to come back from the dead and live. Nope, nope, not even debatable. I must return, please Lord, at least until my baby becomes an adult at eighteen. The angel of death told me to wait on the jasmine petal and sit until he returned. I thought, Huh, how is a flower petal so large that I can sit on it like a chair and wait? The whole time, I kept praying and hoping the Lord would honor my desire to return to my baby.

"When the angel came back, he turned to me and said, 'I have good news, and I have reality news. You will be granted a return to your former life and will see Annabeth Marie grow up, but you will never see your child's thirteenth birthday. Cherish each day like it is your last moment on earth, and live your life, fully enjoying every breath you have been granted extra. Truly, it will be final. The next time I see you will be your return date to our dimension. Next time, your stay here is everlasting as you will not be granted a repeat extension.'

"Constance, my head was spinning, not even thirteen years. How could they shorten my time on my baby's life? But then again, who am I to challenge our Lord when our great God allowed me an extension of life on this earth? Constance, faith does come by hearing the word of God. If you don't believe, then look it up in Isaiah or 2 Kings and see the fifteen years God added to Hezekiah's life when he got sick—cried and prayed! Don't you ever give up believing that He will make a way for you in this lifetime, and He will allow you to complete your destiny of publishing those three books, or my death will have been in vain. Sister, I personally will come and disturb your sleep every day of your life if you don't complete those books for the world to read and grow from.

"Constance, back to the hospital crisis I was in; I quickly came to as they were announcing 'She is gone,' but then I gasped, alerting the closest nurse that maybe I wasn't gone after all.

"Bam! After fifteen minutes departed, I was breathing again, and they started working quickly to get my vitals back in gear. You know, I know I am a miracle, and so is Annabeth Marie, and now, I have just a few short years to impact my child's world in such a positive way that she will never give up on life and she will live for both of us, being the best that she can be. I already know she will have developmental issues caused by her being rapidly pulled out of her dead mother's womb. But as God is my witness, my child will be as normal as can be. No excuses for not achieving her highest potential and doing her best in life to have a productive and meaningful one. I want her to succeed and be happy, and by God, she will do it! She will be adopted by a loving, God-serving family that truly believes in miracles and lives their best lives fully. I asked the angels to ensure that my child can have the opportunity to live with a family that believes in the great 'I AM' of this universe, same as me, and I was told it shall be granted. Her family will be a positive environment that truly believes in our Lord's ability to turn a mustard seed of faith into wonderous miracles. Nothing in this life will be as important as knowing our God's unconditional love and grace. Family will be important to them, as shall be love and goodness."

"Elizabeth Marie, out of all the things that have been foretold, I am dumbfounded this one thing that was to be my destiny was taken from me, and you lived it instead. How in the world does that work? I don't understand. Mami explained these very details you are talking about. To me, it would be me going through this, and instead, it is you. Please tell me why I wasn't the one to give birth to a child? And I did not die and come back? Instead, it is like you took my place. Of all of us, you did not deserve this path after all the calamity of child abuse you had to endure."

"Constance, since I see more than you do and see ahead, I prayed, and God granted the swap. You see, of the two of us, you are the stronger. You are healthier, you can work longer in life, you are pursuing a higher education, you are capable of traveling, you are a fighter, you are not afraid to be in public even though I know you suffer from similar post-traumatic stress disorder issues as I do. Honestly, the Lord will do anything within reason with supplication and prayer, if you are willing to humble yourself before Him. He allowed me to take your place because my life is to be taken sooner, yet it will be extended almost thirteen years longer than what was originally my fate. Isn't that miraculous?"

"No, Elizabeth Marie, I have not ever heard of that before, swapping fates and life being extended. How is it fair when I wanted a child as much as you did, and you were the one granted that privilege? I walk away with just having to write three stupid books about our family's misfortune and historical mess-ups. How in the hell is that a positive in my life?"

"Constance, you had better crack the Bible open and begin reading scripture because it is in there. Begin with studying about Jacob in Genesis when he wrestles with God and gets blessed. We serve a mysterious and mighty God, and His mercy and grace are beyond our capacity to understand. Remember, His ways are not our ways. They are so much more and above what we can ever envision! Sister, I am so sorry now that I did not speak to you at first, but I already knew I was the one to be chosen to die first, and I desperately wanted a child;

a little girl to raise and love. Someone that I could treasure and protect like no one ever did for us." Now Elizabeth Marie is crying uncontrollably. "I am so sorry for my selfishness thinking you'd understand that I had to have this baby girl, a little life of my own to spend time with on this earth, to cherish and love beyond myself. I don't understand why you can't have your own child too. I am so sorry. Please forgive me because you love children so much and will not be allowed to have your own. I don't understand it either."

"Shhh, Elizabeth Marie. I love you beyond myself and would die for you. May the Lord grant as He has set in motion, and may He bless you with pure happiness for your duration on this earth so that you may truly know goodness on this earth. Tell me this, sister. Do you honestly believe the Lord will take you before your child, my niece, is thirteen?"

"Yes, I believe that it can be any time prior to the age of thirteen, so I must treat each day as if it is our last day together. I will treasure and grab life in full force and just choose to be blessed and content. Constance, do you think I am weird with my death story?"

"Not at all, but it makes me wonder my path in life. How does it change since you have lived through what I considered to be a part of my destiny?"

"One more thing, Constance. I should have told you that I was in a coma for nine days before I died. There, I said it all. I am sorry that I am now telling you this, and don't act like you tell me everything because I know that you have been holding something back from me, and I have been patiently waiting for you to tell me because I am your sister and I love you."

Sighing heavily, Constance told Elizabeth Marie that she had just gotten clearance from her endocrinologist. She had been waiting for this moment for years. "Elizabeth Marie, you are right. I have been seeing a specialist for over five years, and well, the worst is over, so I can tell you about it now. I barely had the money to pay for the MRIs and medication required to deal with my issues, plus having to figure out ways to make extra cash to complete a ton of doctor visits and do the therapeutic stuff that I needed to bring my body into a place of peace and better health."

"Tell me, Constance, what was wrong with you?"

"Elizabeth Marie, don't be telling the whole world because it is over now. I must go back in six months for an exit review and one final release from my specialist. I had a tumor underneath my brain that was blocking my pituitary gland and causing me to lactate like a pregnant woman and to gain a ton of weight that I was not able to lose. It also brought about migraines from hell and other body issues that I don't care to discuss. We chose the least invasive route of therapy and healing. It included food choices such as removing processed foods and sugar from my diet and taking the prescribed medication authorized by my health care professional. I couldn't afford to do the surgery, and it would have been too much to do alone and beyond my current budget, so I chose the longer route of five to seven years of shrinking the tumor. It has taken a little over five years, but the tumor is gone, and I am better. I didn't want to worry anyone, so I just kept it to myself."

Elizabeth Marie was crying on the phone. "I just don't know what I would do without you Constance. Please don't hide anything from me EVER again. I pray for you daily, and that is something that I truly can do—pray for your recovery. I love you and only want the best for you. Please, let's not keep secrets from one another. Life is too short to not make the most by living today to the upmost best life possible, and Constance, we don't need to be going through life alone. Promise me, you will tell me everything."

"Okay, baby girl, I will tell you everything, but you must do the same because I will pray for you also, but I must know details, even if it scares you for me to know, promise you will be honest!"

From that day forward, we called each other even more than before, two or three times a week, just to talk and see how things were going. Nothing was ever a secret between us. We'll save our hoarding issues and failed marriages for another time, but yes, even hard topics were covered. At times, we would fuss at each other, and other times, we would give advice. Sometimes, we would just watch something on television jointly and discuss the outcome. At times, we would listen to music and pick apart the meaning of the words. Many times, we were going over the details of Elizabeth Marie's beautiful baby girl. How Annabeth Marie is moving and growing, what clothes she is wearing, her favorite toys, especially the panda bears, swimming, and her love of talking, and activities for motor and cognitive play. We'd dissect the therapies she was taking to assist with her developmental adjustments. Often, we would review her early intervention therapy reports by reading and sharing what we thought the therapists were trying to say. Elizabeth Marie would make a list of follow-up questions for the therapists. In addition, Elizabeth Marie has been preparing me by promising to give her baby girl her ashes and stuff she has given me through the years and telling her daughter anything she may wish to know about her or her past, but only if Annabeth Marie inquires and/or is curious about anything that has to do with her.

In our existence, we have had the best of times just being sisters. Laughing, crying, nurturing one another, and praying together, we are connected deeper than two souls lost in the thicket of a dense and endless forest that has not ever been discovered by any well-traveled explorer. We love each other so much may nothing ever come between us and tear us apart.

Chapter 13

Papi Search

The phone was ringing nonstop, but Constance was tired and heading toward the back bathroom to take a shower. No time to be bothered. Yet, after the seventh round of nonstop ringing, she went over to see who it was. It was Sandrida, and she rarely called, let alone back-to-back calls, so Constance sat down and called her right back.

"Sandrida, are you alright? I can't even get a shower in because the phone is ringing off the hook. What is going on?"

"Constance, we found him. WE FOUND HIM!"

"Oh." Constance knew instantly who Sandrida was referring to. "What makes you believe that you have found him?"

"Okay, so the kids, [her own], a set of twenty-year-old twins, were surfing the internet, and there was this article from a nursing home about him, and I looked at the photo they posted… then, we called and showed it to Francisco. However, he won't say anything about it either way, stated he will have to look into it, but the way he said it, I just know that he knows that it is him!"

"Slow down, Sandrida. Who is they, and what photo?"

"I think he is in a nursing home, and I just sent you the picture. Look at it and see if you think it looks like our sister, Elizabeth Marie. We saw this article from a nursing home posted on social media, and it talked about him in detail. He was in a nursing home near Austin, Texas. Sounds like he has been there a little over a year. Can you go see if it is him? Can you call the nursing home tomorrow and see if it is him? In the article, it says he was Resident of the Month."

Sighing, Constance knew the time had come. Mami had predicted this long ago, and she did not want to go through with it, but it was destiny and to get on the completed healing side of her past with their dad, whom they all still called, "Papi," which means daddy in Spanish, she would have to follow through with her part. "Give me a minute, Sandrida. Let me take a look, and I will call you back in five minutes."

Getting off the phone, Constance looked at the photo that was sent to her, and sure enough, staring before her was Papi. Undeniably, he was the spitting image of their sister, Elizabeth Marie. Constance's nose looking right back at her with those deep, dark, sad brown eyes and a hint of 'something' reflecting mysteriously into a disturbed bygone. Quickly, Constance looked for his arms and saw the prison tattoos of a Texas longhorn and what was supposed to have had a dream catcher in between the longhorns. The forehead area of the longhorn ended up looking more like the body of a guitar rather than the intended vision. It was the recognizable tracing of a thin outline of an idea that was never completed. Yup, looking at the photo, it was unquestionably their Papi.

Constance called Sandrida back, and they decided to contact their sister Magdelina to see if she was good with reaching out to this man that they believed to be their Papi. Constance told Sandrida to ring Magdelina and to let her know in twenty minutes their decision because she was going to take a quick shower.

Precisely twenty minutes later, Sandrida called elated. Magdelina was all in to having Constance contact the nursing home where they believed their Papi resided.

Long pause. Sandrida sighed. "Okay, so I know I have heard that he was not the best father, nor was he even a good person at times or around enough to be considered a doting dad, but I need this more than anything. Constance, you and Magdelina have memories of him, and I have nothing. I was so young that I can't even remember what he looked like. I can't see his face or tattoos that you two describe. I see nothing." Sandrida was crying. "I can't hear his voice, let alone recall him taking us to the park to play or him mowing the lawn. All I know is that we four girls are his daughters, and he was married to our Mami. Please call and see if it is him. Do this for me. I can't call because I can't fathom the thought of it not being him. Worst yet, if it is him, and he denies he has kids. What would I say to him, and what questions would I ask to confirm that he is our dad?"

"Sandrida, I will do this for all of us, but just know there could be a slim possibility that it may not be him, but you would know that we tried. For your sake, I hope that it is him because he may have gotten his life together by now, and maybe he has prayed that we would find him. Either way, we will get through this together. I love you, baby girl, and want this opportunity for you to connect with him. On the other hand, do not ask me to meet you to go see him at the nursing home or anywhere else because I don't ever want to see him in person ever again. I don't have to because, legally, he is not my father anymore, and I am good with that. Even though I forgave him long ago for my own sake and sanity, I still know deep down in my heart what he did to me and how much hate I had to stomach from him. It was more loathing than any child should have had to deal with. But if he found God and got himself together, then you should get the chance to reconnect with him.

"Sandrida, give me a few days. I must pray about this and mentally prepare myself for anything. I want you to pray, too. Please pray that I say the words needed now and that I respond to him appropriately. Also implore that I have the wisdom to control my emotions and the intelligence to structurally say what needs to be spoken to reconnect with a person that I never wish to see again in my life. Because Mami told my future, I already know this is Papi, and we will make peace before he dies, and I will be the one to identify him for legal purposes so his death certificate can be completed. Mami gave me information they will need when he passes. I will also be the one who will write his obituary. Sandrida, start saving your money because you will come to see him and get to spend the time that you long for with him."

Sandrida was gasping. "Constance, do you honestly believe everything that Mami tells you is true?"

"Yes, Mami has not ever been wrong or misleading. Sometimes, I have not cared for her predictions, and at times, it has been painful to know the truth before it happens. I don't understand how telling the future helps people. Why can't we just let life happen? Still, just like this situation, I am always surprised when the time of the prediction finally comes about and happens just the way that she foretold it. I think, damn, she was right yet again. I love you, Sandrida. I will talk to you in a few days."

"Constance, I know this is not easy for you. Just know I will light a candle and pray. I love you, too. Talk later."

Chapter 14

Straight Talk

"Medical Nursing Home and Resort of Round Rock, how may I assist you?"

At eight in the evening, Constance was thinking she had procrastinated long enough and should probably call now or never. She already knew how it would turn out, and she was good with it. "Good evening. I am trying to reach my father, Freddy, or he may go by Slim, who is currently staying there. Please tell him that Constance, his second oldest living child, is on the phone."

"Miss, my name is Michelle, and I am looking at the visitor and contact logs, and I do not see you on the list."

"Michelle, if you know my dad, you already know that he has spoken of his wife, who was an awesome cook, and how he wishes to see his four daughters and stepson."

"I will have to go and speak with him and see if he is willing to converse with you. If his answer is yes, then I will call you back in ten minutes."

What seemed like eternity, ten minutes later, Constance received a call from the nursing home with Michelle's sunshiny voice, declaring, "Constance, he is here and ready to speak with you. I will add you, your sisters, and brother to the list so that you may contact him whenever you wish. He has been here over a year, and you are the first person who has called him. Our social worker on staff will be delighted to know that family has reached out. Please come to visit and spend time here. You are welcome day or night. He is on the resident phone, and his daily limit is thirty minutes. However, since he has never used any of his time, go ahead, and you two may speak however long you would like since most of the residents are sleeping."

"Hello, this is Freddy. No one has called me Slim in decades. Tell me who this is and why you are calling me at a nursing home. How do I know that you are not an imposter?"

"Are you serious right now? The lady just told me that you have been there for over a year, and I am the first person to call or even inquire about you. Whom but your own children would even be seeking to look for you? I wouldn't even be calling except that your youngest daughter can hardly remember what you look like and has no clue what an ass and useless piece of shit you were when you drank, were abusive, and left your family, just to come back and try to be a family man all over again, but that never lasted long, did it? Mami loved you with all her heart, and she kept letting you come back to try again, until she finally divorced your ass. So, you know in your heart that I am your daughter, and I speak the truth. You already know that I know it is you because I recognize your voice, and I have seen your Resident of the Month photo and your tattoos. Elizabeth Marie looks exactly like you, and there is no denying that we are your children. I still have your nose, and Magdelina is your spitting image, just slightly darker than you. Papi, I am the daughter that you never claimed."

"Why are you calling me Papi? You are a grown woman calling me Daddy. Don't you think that is odd?"

"Papi is all that I have ever known you as, but if you just want me to call you Freddy, then I can do that, and I don't have a problem calling you 'Hey you' if you prefer that."

"Well, you were always white and always in the way."

"Papi, get this straight in your head, or you won't hear from me again. I know that you have found God and seek to reconnect with your children. I already know that in my spirit, so do not lie to me and do not play games with me. We will be honest with each other because Mami has made sure that I am informed about you—her lover, the father of her children. I also know the whole truth about you, to every final detail of what happened that night when your drinking went all wrong, so wake up and know that there are no secrets. Let's try this again. You tell me the truth of how you ended up in this nursing home because we all know that you have an alcoholic addiction that would keep you on the streets until your last breath. Unless you found Jesus or something traumatic happened that would force you into confinement, such as a nursing home or hospital? It would have to be out of your control to be here, so talk and spit out the truth."

"Damn girl, you don't bullshit around. You are most definitely related to me in that sense. You have your mother's voice which brings me so many sentimental and bittersweet memories. You are right about my drinking. Been doing too much of that since my teenage years, and it just got worse as I got older. You know, I truly love my wife and children with all my heart, just couldn't break the drinking thing and I was forced into the nursing home against my will. Hell, I can't even have one goddamn beer with my meals, and I am a grown ass man."

Constance caught the sarcasm in his voice, "It is not a part of the diabetic's nutritional meal, so I must do without, says the nutritionist on staff." A pause, and then, "Anyway, what happened was one cold night, I remember having to put on my Salvation Army heavy coat, which was just given to me the day before in preparation for the cold weekend. I guess I passed out with half of my body in Town Lake, with the bed of water streaming slowly due to the extreme cold. Don't ask me how I got there because I had been over by the cemetery on Seventh Street, near the railroad tracks hoping I'd run into your Mami just to say hello to her and see how she was doing. Well, I had my lower half in the water and the other half on the bank. Apparently, in a nest of water moccasins—you know, the poisonous snakes of Texas. Imagine the scare of the shotgun rounds I heard near me and the siren of the ambulance as I regained consciousness. I barely remember being pulled out of the freezing cold stream before I passed out again. Next thing I know, I was in this goddamn place trying to figure out a way to leave. Long story. Short version: I had been bitten by two water moccasins, and how they know it was two beats the hell out of me, but they had to chop my legs off and, well, here I am, stuck in this godforsaken place for the rest of my life. The crazy thing about all of this is that because I was three sheets to the wind, drunk out of my mind, the alcohol and freezing cold weather had reduced my heart and blood flow so slow that it was what saved my life. Damn! Who knew my addiction would keep me alive one day? Isn't that ironic?"

Constance just starts laughing and laughing.

"What the hell, girl? Why are you laughing? Don't you see I am stuck here forever, and I can never have another drink in my life."

"Freddy, you know that God has a way of answering our prayers and making us face our demons of the past so that He can make way for our goodness, and here you are."

"Well, hell, a drink now and again shouldn't be such a bad thing. Besides, now that I don't drink, I'm having the worst nightmares and rarely sleep like a normal person. Most of the time, I catnap here and there. Goddamn it, when I do sleep, I don't rest, and it seems like life is such a waste, just living day to day praying I will die before the next torturous round of nightmares consumes my mind."

"Papi, you prayed that your girls would find you, and how did you expect us to do that if you are still on the streets? I did look for you over a year ago on Seventh Street in Austin, where you used to hang out, but I was told you had moved to Rockwall, Texas and there I could never find you. Now, years later, you were found on the internet because your nursing staff wrote a piece on the Resident of the Month, and it was all about you. You talked about your wife and daughters. Honestly, how else were we to locate you? Because I bet you have been homeless most of your life?"

"Damn girl, what do you know about homelessness? I wouldn't trade my street family for anything; they have been my family, and we have had each other's best interests for decades. They are probably upset now because I am not on the streets, and they can't find me because they just took me and dumped me here. Do you know it is safer on the streets than at the Salvation Army housing? Because there they steal from you while you sleep, and out here, we take turns and sleep and cover for each other. We get odd jobs and work when we can, but mostly, we know the system that has food, clothes, showers, and on occasion, we'd choose jail time just to get away from it all, even if just for a weekend. So don't knock it. Once my marriage failed with your Mami, and she didn't want me to come around drunk to spend time with you kids, well, I had nothing to live for. So my world revolved around my street family. It was a good one: hopping trains traveling America, figuring out ways to make it, enjoying God's nature and camping. It was just not the traditional way of doing things, but it has been good, and I love my street family."

Constance encouraged him, "Tell me more."

"You are correct. I lost touch with all of my brothers and parents half a century ago, in my early twenties, because my family life growing up was not the easiest."

"Papi, I heard your sister Marie died young. I am sorry."

"Stop it. You know, if your Mami told you the truth about my past, you already know your Tia Marie was never my sister. My parents had fourteen boys, and it is the reason that my mother drank herself to an early grave, because she could never have a girl. You know, she was only fifty when she died."

"Then why did Marie grow up with you?"

"The neighbor lady felt so bad for my parents that she agreed to give them one of her daughters, Marie. They were neighbors all their lives, so it's not like Marie didn't know because we kids told her that she belonged next door. Besides, Marie grew up with both families. Anyway, the reason I started drinking heavily is because your grandmother was so inebriated most of her existence, and since I was the oldest, I had to raise the kids. Just think I am seven; cooking, cleaning, changing diapers, doing everything a mother should do while she went through life passed out with her cigarettes and alcohol near her stand. She never cared about anything except trying to make baby girls, and my dad was too busy working just to put food on the table to help her snap out of her misery. If I didn't help her, she would beat me until I bled, and I'd rather she beat me than my younger brothers. It wasn't our fault they never had girls. It was always the reason that I hated boys so much.

"When I met your Mami, she already had one kid, and it was a boy. Yeah, I didn't want him anywhere around me, and eventually, he went to the ranch to be raised by your great-grandmother and great uncles. Through the grapevine, I heard that he ended up mostly being raised by your Mami's favorite cousin, Patsy."

"Papi, you don't get a free pass. I already know about not letting Mami change Francisco's diapers. It was so bad he often had maggots in between the diaper and his legs. Don't think I don't already know about you putting Francisco in between two mattresses and how you attempted to smother him to death. What the hell made you do that?"

"As an alcoholic, I just wanted him to go away because he was yet another boy I did not want to raise and take care of, but your Mami loved him and me so much. I gave her an ultimatum that I would have to leave, or Francisco would have to go elsewhere."

"You really are a sick person and deserve to rot in hell."

"You don't have to forgive me, but I asked God into my life a few years ago and just want my old age to be better than my younger years. I want to do better, and yes, I did pray to reconnect with your Mami and my kids before I died. I have been busy working on my plan and getting myself in a better frame of mind these past few years. I even finished high school by getting my GED. Then I went to school to become a chef and was a cook off and on when I wanted to work. But seriously, I hated being around people and their stupidity, so I'd get into brawls, and then I'd get fired because people do not know how to shut up with their incompetent ideas. To me, it was worth being terminated after I cussed somebody off or beat the shit out of some asshole who deserved it."

"Freddy, I already know the answer, but go ahead and tell me your version of the story because I want to know it. I am a girl, and yet, you were horrible to me and hated me; what was that all about?"

"Well, if you already know, then why dig up the past?"

"Because you owe me that much. The truth."

"Fine, but I can't change the past. It is over: bad or ugly. Your sister was only three months old, and I barely recall that night."

Irritated, Constance belted out, "Whatever. You remember enough to know you were in the wrong."

"I had had a bad day at work, and now the baby had run out of formula, and she was not feeding well on breast milk, so she just cried and cried and wouldn't shut up. Your Mami was going to get more formula, then it happened so fast, and before I knew it, the baby was on the floor and gone. Your Mami was screaming to get help, and I couldn't console her, so I just left. I told her if she truly loved me, she'd say she did it. We could make another baby."

"No fucking way am I hearing what you just said to be true. Do you hear how heartless and what an idiotic ass you sound like right now? 'We could make another baby'."

"Anyway, your Mami paid the price, and she was put away because she couldn't cope with the reality of losing her baby girl, and that was the beginning of the end of our relationship. Nothing could ever go back to the way that it was. We tried. The Lord knows we tried. I mean, we had three more daughters after her. Damn you for being born on her birthday nine months later. Why did you have to look exactly like her but a very white version of her. I could never get rid of you, and I resented the fact that you would never let me forget what happened that night."

"I was a child, and it's not my fault what date I was born on and who I resembled.

"The fact that you are still alive tells me why I have my nightmares."

"Freddy, I forgave you long ago, not for your sake but for mine. I needed to be set free from my past and move on, and I had to forgive you, not forget, but to let go of your horrible ways toward me just so that I could move on with my life. Let me tell you something: your nightmares? They won't go away. Nope. Not until you are ready to move beyond this life. When you are ready, you must begin to tell the truth about what happened. Yes, like selling me to men to be molested for your bottles of whiskey. Don't think I have forgotten what you did to me, and it wasn't because you were drunk. It was because you were an asshole and cruel. Tell the truth to whomever will listen about yourself and what really happened in your world. Alcohol and the pretense of a different life cannot erase what you did."

"Who in the hell cares about what happened decades ago?"

"Freddy, you know the truth, and hiding now behind what you did is what is causing your visions; begin with telling your social worker. Back then, shaken baby syndrome wasn't a thing, and they did not send you to jail for it, but God knows the truth, and it is time you confess and be honest with yourself. Trust me, you will continue to grow old and will not be released from your hallucinations until you are honest with yourself. Then and only then will you find peace and the Lord will take you. Remember that when you can't sleep at night and don't have alcohol to drown your sorrows and your lies. Remember how you didn't have any problem letting Mami go to jail and to the insane asylum for you? That wasn't love. You don't show love by allowing someone to spend time in jail or mental institutions for you.

"You are just a piss-poor coward and one who still does not have the guts to go to the police to let them know that it was you and not Mami who did what you did, all because, in a drunken condition, you couldn't stand your own child's cry for food. That baby was hungry, and you ended her life, just because she was an infant, acting like an infant. Yes, babies cry when they are hungry, and you had no right to grab her and throw her to the ground to shut her up. Fuck you, and may you rot in your own misery of nightmares. You can't fool me. You will not ever find empathy here when you can't even be honest with yourself. Your bad dreams are your opportunity to ask for forgiveness and to quit waddling in your own pity. You had no right to take another's life just because your own childhood was horrible.

"I wasn't going to tell you this, but Mami foretold our conversation long ago and part of my assignment is to relay her messages to the people on her list—the people that she loved the most. You are one of them, so listen. You don't have to tell me what you think, nor do you have to believe what I am telling you but let me get this message out so that I can check it off my list."

Gazing wide-eyed, Papi looked straight at his phone in disbelief. "Constance, she didn't tell you when I would die, did she? You know everything she predicts does come true, right?"

"Listen, Freddy. Here is her message to you." Constance took a deep breath. "'My love, the father of five of my children, I forgave you long ago, and now you must forgive yourself. Your life has not ever been easy, but punishing yourself for what was out of your control is not the way to keep going. You chose alcohol as your slow suicide, your prison to carry around with you wherever you go. When you repented before Christ, you were forgiven as far as the east is from the west, so quit plucking your sins from the depths of the unforgiven just to replay what was the past over and over. Let it go and live only for today. You will see some of your children, your grandchildren, and even a great-grandchild. Consider yourself more fortunate than most. Celebrate those moments. When your time comes, I will be waiting for you. You will find it interesting that even though you were homeless, you will have a proper burial site, and eventually, your family will visit you and lay you down to rest. Constance has been given information about your parents, and she will write your obituary. Your peace will come with telling and releasing your truths that you have kept hidden. Only then will you be ready to cross over.'"

Freddy just stared at the phone in skepticism, but he knew his wife had a gift that never failed her. Tears brimming over his eyelids, he could hear himself, voice cracking, "Thank you, Constance, you don't know what this means to me. I-I-I am so sorry I took it all out on you, and I want you to know it was never you, the kid, my child, that I was pissed off at. It was me and not being able to get my shit together to have a normal family life. I loved your Mami so much and wanted to be a family man, but just couldn't ever do it. I was always too busy feeling sorry for myself and how my mother treated me, and no one ever came to save me from my hurts. I never learned how to move beyond the pain of rejection and child abuse. Instead, I chose alcohol to bury my hurt, and in the process, I lost everything that should have been good in my life. Daughter, may you choose to live life to the fullest beyond your pain and rejection."

"Listen, Freddy. I had wonderful people in my life; my foster parents taught me how to deal with grief, and they taught me that I come from an exceptional birth family that just had too many personal issues that were beyond their own pain to process. My foster parents taught me to allow the God of the Universe to wrap His arms around me and heal my heart and then to turn around and bless others who have experienced similar grief as myself. Like I said, you were forgiven long ago, and now it is your turn to face grief, forgive, and move on. If you wish to communicate with me by phone, then I will call you periodically, but I will not ever visit you. The others do wish to see you again. What are your thoughts on that?"

"I get that you don't want to see me ever again, but I am thankful that you are even willing to speak with me. Tell your sisters and brother that I do wish to see them if they are willing. Francisco, too, if he is willing to see me. I understand that because of the way that I treated him, he may never want to see me either, but I want to ask his forgiveness in person because I was so wrong and evil. There are no excuses for what I did. Constance, do I have any grandchildren?"

"Yes, but I will let each of your children share their own stories because I value privacy, and I believe that if they wish to tell you anything personal, then it is their story to tell."

"Fair enough. Constance, I honestly believed that you were not my child. However, listening to you talk now, I know that I can't deny that you are mine. Even if you choose to never speak with me again, thank you for talking with me today. I am glad you shared your Mami's words and did not hold back your feelings because you are right in my head. I fantasize about my family and create my own happy place of the perfect family. Now, it is time to face reality and process my real experiences. With most of my hardships, I should have pushed myself to do more and be a better person. I created my own hell because I was reprimanding myself for all my mistakes. Alcohol was my cheapest way out. The bad thing is it took more and more, and then stronger and stronger liquor, through the years to make me escape the present, and they say it made me a meaner drunk. No excuses. Becoming sober lately has really messed me up in the head because I have no more escapes to turn to, and my nightmares are brutal. I wake up scared, covered in sweat, and all I do is cry and hurt. The pain is unbearable. So, thank you again for sharing your Mami's message."

"Freddy, I will call again and ask questions about you and your family, but I must process today's conversation. It is a lot of information for a two-hour chat. Still, I will wait a few weeks and call again. Just let Michelle and your social worker know we will each be calling, and some of my siblings will visit."

"Okay, talk later."

"Bye, Freddy. Talk later."

Truth be told, Francisco and I had already filed a police report on Freddy long ago. Research had taught us that back in the day, shaken baby syndrome was not a thing, and neither was going to jail for it. Mami had been put in a mental institution to cope with what had taken place. And the fact that she had told the police that she did it, then later came back and told the truth, well, that did not change anything other than sealed a date for our parents' divorce. Mami would walk the streets, cast spells to call up her baby girl, and then go by the river where the baby had allegedly been thrown into that fatal night. Then she would cry for forgiveness until she made herself sick, or someone would call the cops to come and see what was going on. Through the years that I'd come to Austin, Texas, to visit, at least every other visit, Mami would have me take her to the cemetery to speak with her baby. She would cry, light candles, place flowers on her tomb, and ask forgiveness. Then she would say, "I will see you soon and see your wholeness. I love you beyond the grave and can't wait to have you in my arms."

Afterward, she would want to go home and sleep deeply until the following day.

For me, it will forever be a sad moment in our family's history that never should have happened, and I hope others will choose never to harm a child much less one who is helpless and dependent on parents, yes, adults for everything.

Yes, there were other conversations with Freddy through the years, and it is true; time does heal old wounds, but the mind and heart never forget. We made our peace, and ultimately, Freddy chose to tell his truths and make his peace. He once told me that in the end, the only thing that matters is relationships and telling the truth or just plainly manning up and being sincere with oneself. He was grateful God allowed him to reconnect with his children because ultimately, it was what set him free and would propel him into the afterlife.

Chapter 15

Vino's Last Stand

At a social worker's dream convention in Austin, Texas, around January 2004, I received a call to let me know that Tio Vino was in a nursing home and hospice was involved. It wouldn't be long before my uncle's end would be here and he would be gone. I already knew, as one of my most active abusers during childhood, I was to spend time with him before his crossing to the eternal. Still, did I want to do this or not? *He is Mami's brother and, in ways, special to me.* He is, after all, my uncle who took me to see my first movie, *Snow White and the Seven Dwarfs,* and my first carnival ride. He made sure to encourage me as I got on the boats and bumper cars. He was the main one who abused me and Elizabeth Marie when we were little. He was caught by Mami when he was attempting full penetration with me. I never understood why he was allowed to be around us, even if other adults were present, knowing what he did to children. I just have so many mixed emotions about this uncle, and yet, I mourn that his time on earth is short. What an odd dichotomy to process through, but I chose to see my uncle one last time.

January 11, 2004. Tio Vino is dying of cancer that has spread to his brain, lungs, and kidneys. He won't live too much longer. He is in incredible pain. Knocking at his door, he calls out "Mija, come in. I knew you would come and, like your Mami used to, I speak with the dead. Your Mami has told me to listen and take heed to your words and for me to share my story with you as well."

In a chair near my uncle is my favorite uncle, Petro. We hugged. How I adore this man. He never once touched me wrong when I was a child. He made sure when he was in the area that he had food, clothing, and toys for us children. He would come with his wife, Luna. She would brush our hair and make sure our clothes were washed and presentable. Tia/Aunt Luna would say, "I made too much food at home and don't want to throw it away, and I know my babies here will love the fresh tortillas, potatoes, and refried beans. Oh, and our kids are tired of bananas, apples, and oranges, so you kids can eat the rest." We would just jump for joy as Tia Luna would take the food to the kitchen and separate it in piles for each of us to last for several days. Such great memories.

Many years later my Tia Luna told me to my face that she was so proud of me and how I grew up to be the good girl she prayed that I would be: educated, resourceful, funny, and a quick thinker. She knows in her heart even though it had been a shock to the family when we were snatched that night, and no one had a clue where we had gone, and later found out that we had all been adopted, except for the oldest boy, that it was wise we had been removed because it gave us all an opportunity for a better life rather than staying with Mami in a toxic and unsafe environment.

Mami had also told her that she was so proud of her babies, how we each had grown up smart and with a safe upbringing. She knew she herself would not have been able to protect us from harm and provide the same level of care we all desperately needed. Mami let go of her children because she knew she was unstable and mentally unhealthy. It was never because she quit loving her children. Every day, she would see Tia Luna and ask her to believe, pray, and meditate for her children that they were safe and happy. I remember telling my Tia, I always knew in my heart that Mami's love ran deeper than the blood that rushes through my veins to keep me alive and I will always love and respect Mami for letting go.

Back to the present. Tio Vino, I see, is slumped over; the only thing keeping him in his wheelchair are the restraining bands. The left side of his body is drooping. Tio Petro shares he is not eating, refuses to drink, and he appears lost in his thoughts.

Tio Vino takes a deep breath and focuses on me. "Constance, you have come, and I am grateful. You know your Mami loves you with all of her being. Constance, please get me some cold water." He is aware and agrees to be placed back on his bed so he can be zoomed up into a better sitting position. He states, "I want to see you, child, and since I can't control my body anymore, being on the bed is the best place for me to see you."

Situated on the bed, he agrees to take his last photo with me. Then, I take the envelope I brought with me and take out the photos of my uncles' parents, my grandparents, along with reprints of Mami. They both start to cry. They both thought no one had any photos of their parents and family anymore. Then they both take turns and speak of the past, smiling with tears of joy. They recalled how wealthy and strong they were when they were young.

How can life go so wrong? Out of the five children that their parents had, well, four, they are the only ones alive. After their dad died was when they found out that the eldest child was a product of incest, but their dad gave him his last name and raised him as his own. The youngest died first in a fatal car accident when he was eighteen years old. Mami was the next to pass in 2001, and now Uncle Vino is soon to cross the great divide. Tio Petro and I look at each other and nod toward Tio Vino; he is sound asleep.

Tio Petro and I go and find some food to eat, then we go to the nearest Walmart to shop for a few necessities. While I drive, Tio Petro smiles at me and stutters, "Co – n – st – stance, your Mami would be so proud of you. Thank you for being here. I love you for coming back to this hell and being here."

I tell him, "You were always good to me and my siblings, and I want to thank you for that. I am glad you are here today."

As we pass the Catholic and Methodist churches that are a part of our family traditions, he makes a cross in front of him and tells me, "When we pass the church, you must make a cross and respect the Church. Jesus is the only way to anything. When Vino is gone, you can turn to the Church for everything—your loneliness and for strength. It is what has kept me going all these years and what has led me back to this place."

I look at him and share, "For the sake of history, and for the sake of family; I know so much because you, Mami, and so many have been willing to share and keep me in the family, even though, legally, I am not."

"Constance, papers and the law cannot strike out the blood that runs through your veins. You are forever one of us. Our surnames on both sides of our family have roots in this land that run through the ages. You have so much to be proud of. Just in our neighborhood are real estate properties that used to be owned by my dad and his family. There is a motel on Seventh Street, barber shops, restaurants, and even one of our cousins is in politics, not to mention the pastors in the churches are all related to us. We have a huge family from here to San Antonio, New Orleans, Mexico City, Spain, Mexico, and even Italy. Never forget where you come from. Begin with the streets in Austin that my dad named after the ships of Columbus that our ancestors traveled with. Our family history is full of pride, power, and prosperity, such humble beginnings of the working farmer and customer service. The young people do not take the time to know the truth. They just see the bad that it's become. Constance, tell our story. It is a good one. How I miss my parents."

The next day, I saw my Tio Vino several times. He tells me to honor my dad and at least go and find him. He is on the streets of Austin and goes to the Salvation Army and a few other homeless outreach programs off Ceasar Street to eat and sleep. He has been asking for his daughters and wants to ask forgiveness; "Give him that opportunity to do right by you."

"Tio Vino, you are on your last days of life on earth, and you want me to forgive my dad?"

"Constance, we all need a chance in life to do right and be forgiven, even if we really don't deserve it."

"Tio Vino, I know what you did to me when I was fourteen months old, and I also know what you did to Elizabeth Marie. Plus, what you have been doing to Mami all these years is not a secret."

He begins to weep and exclaims, "Constance, do not go to the police with this. They will put me away. I am so sorry. I was wrong, and my choices of the past are cruel and evil. Constance, I can't think of the past. I must get ready to move on …. I really did those things to you, and I am so sorry now. I see on this bed that I was wicked and wrong."

Then, out of nowhere, he yells, "Where was anyone to save me when I was being butt fucked by my uncle? No one spared me, no one heard my cries, and sure as hell, no mother of mine made sure I was safe. You tell me, where were my protectors and rescuers?"

Slumping forward, I reach out and hug him. We cry together for a long time.

"Tio Vino, Elizabeth Marie and I forgave you long ago. Go to your new place knowing you are forgiven by us, and we love you. Me going to the police should be the least of your worries. It is the Almighty, the great I Am that you will have to account to, so I would recommend you turn your eyes and heart to him. It is not me you should be concerned about; I am in the past, and so are all those haunting moments of your meanness."

"Child, I am so glad that you are here. I know God, too, will accept my request for forgiveness. I see now even as my body soars in pain, and even though I beg God to take me, he prolonged my life to see you once more. For it is destiny that we part ways with an understanding: your necessity to face me about your truths about what I tried to do to you as a baby and those other times later when I did molest you as a child and caused horrific tortuous agony with the malicious physical abuse. I know that I had no right to hurt others because of what happened to me as a child. You also needed to know how deep the roots of incest and abuse are on my mother's side of the family and how imperative it is that it must stop. Say out loud to your generation what happened to me in my generation, and it must stop.

"Constance, you are so much like your Mami: stubborn, brave, kindhearted, and a beautiful person. Never forget how much you look like her. I love you, Constance. You go in peace and know you are loved. I see your Mami now. She loves you beyond the grave. She sees you and is cheering for you. Love never fails. Remember that. Constance, my head is in so much pain, I cannot take anymore. This is all I can talk about right now."

"Tio Vino, I am leaving now. I must go to work tomorrow." I lean over to hug and kiss him, knowing it will be the last time I see him. "Tio Vino, I see that you look like my grandaddy. Did you know that?"

"Yes, I look like my dad, and I have always looked like him. You go now and be careful. Go to your husband and love him. One day, we will meet again, and it will be a joyous reunion."

My uncle Petro and I adjust him on the bed as he falls into a deep slumber. I then hug my Tio Petro goodbye and head home on what appears to be a long ride of reconciliation with the past. Tears streaming, a heavy wet flow of bittersweetness. I, too, must complete the healing process of letting go of that incestuous ugliness and move on with the present.

I call Marisa and just empty my thoughts onto her generous, caring, sisterly ways.

"Connie Jo, I love you and am so proud of you. Your Mami would be proud too."

"Marisa, this completes the long list of men who hurt me. Most of them are dead and gone, with only two alive, of which one of them is still in prison."

"Connie Jo, why chase the dead when you should be chasing the living and choosing life? That is the legacy that you live, wrapping your goodness in the living. It is okay, baby girl, to live in the now and to be happy. You have researched, documented, reconciled and now it is time to enjoy daily living, just like your Mami taught you."

"Marisa, Mami taught me to see the person and the evil, learn to separate the two so that forgiving can happen to release you from the past, and now you are teaching me to live in the now. Thank you so much for helping me to recalculate and refocus on the here and now. To teach me I matter as well. I love you."

"Connie Jo, come and see me when you return to town and bring your puppy, Shelby, so that she can enjoy the swimming pool. I love you, and we shall talk soon. Take away this thought that God's plan for you is good and is not dependent on your past but His promise. He does not give you a plan He will not finish, so move forward and persevere."

Chapter 16

Tucson's Landing

"**M**iss, miss, are you alright? We have landed in Tucson, and people are departing the plane."

Looking up at the beautiful, cheerful flight attendant, Constance quickly thanked her and snapped back to reality, realizing she really was in Tucson, Arizona. Constance gathered her wits about her and grabbed all her belongings. Wiping away the last of her tears, she put some antihistamine drops in both of her eyes because she already knew the desert dust was going to make her sinuses go wild for the next few days. Telling herself to be in the present and go straight to luggage, Constance proceeded to somberly leave the plane with a heavy heart. It was not long before she was smiling and laughing as she saw Sandrida waiting for her in the luggage area, asking her which one was her suitcase so she could grab it and they could go. The twins were in the car waiting for them. Giggling, Constance asked, "Can I at least get my welcoming hug from you before you escort me out of this building?"

Looking at her sheepishly, Sandrida smiled. "Yes, sister, let me hug you and kiss your cheek with Arizona welcomes. I am so happy you came. My goodness, have you eaten? You must be hungry?"

"No, not really. Just been sitting in the plane for hours, thinking about the past and going through so many memories and thoughts of our lives."

Instantly, Sandrida broke down, crying. "I just can't do this alone; I am just so thankful you came and are here. Please tell me what to do and where to begin?"

Hugging one another tightly, both in tears, they calmed each other. "Sandrida, we will get through this together, and we will have our moments of good times, making memories with the children. Let's get my luggage and go."

By now, Constance's luggage had gone around the circuit several times and was one of the few items left on the moving belt. Grabbing her suitcase, they hurried to where the twins were waiting. Hugging the twins and placing the suitcase in the trunk, they were off to Sandrida's house. It was a short distance to their home, and it did not take long to get there. On the way, they drove by Elizabeth Marie's home, and Constance observed the front yard full of multiple furniture pieces, including large appliances. Gazing at Constance, Sandrida said, "I took your advice and decided to go ahead and go through each room of our parents' large home, and we pulled everything we knew we would not ever use and brought those items out for the garage sale. We have already had people stop by the house, and they have already bought stuff before the actual sale. Our parents were horrible about having two of a lot of the same things. We took the well-preserved stuff and left the other items for the rummage sale. Some of the people who have stopped by already are neighbors we have known most of our lives, so we just went ahead and let them go through and get what they wanted before a crowd comes in the morning. It is incredible how much money we have made, and the garage sale is not until tomorrow and Sunday."

On the way to the house, Sandrida had Eric, the younger of the twins, stop by their favorite chicken restaurant to get everyone lunch. He chose chicken, green beans, mashed potatoes, and biscuits. Once at the house, we unloaded everything and freshened up. Then, we all ate lunch and sat around for hours talking. Erica, the oldest twin, kept hugging Constance and wanted to show her photos, while Eric played happy music in the background. It was a good nostalgic afternoon just sharing memories and being together. Later, they were planning to return to Sandrida and Elizabeth Marie's childhood home to look for vital documents that Sandrida would need to give to the bank to settle on the reverse mortgage. Constance had spoken to a bank manager and had already shared with Sandrida that the house belonged to the bank, and it was urgent they went through the house and collected everything they wanted because, after the current month, the bank would take over the house. It was decided only Sandrida and Constance would return to the house today, and tomorrow, everyone would assist with boxing up anything they deemed valuable and necessary to keep.

Prior to leaving the house, Eric whispered and shared, "Tia, I found her, and it was brutal. The instant pain so traumatic that I just can't seem to get it out of my head. It was late at night and the medicine that she keeps by her bed with water, she must have forgotten it in the kitchen because it was like she was reaching for it and water. The bottle of pills had spilled all over the floor with the glass of water broken in the sink. The water was still running when I found her. Called 9-1-1, but I already knew it was too late to save her. It was more about getting our cousin out of the house and over to ours so that she wouldn't see everything going on. I just can't stand the pain, knowing she is gone forever. What kind of God takes away a parent from a twelve-year-old knowing her father is in another country? I just don't get it. Honestly, I just don't know if I will ever believe in a higher being that takes the good loving people from this world only to keep the shitty ones still around. How does that work, and how do you expect me to believe everything happens for a reason? Just sucks, and I hate everything right now because she was my favorite Tia; my world, my everything and now gone, never to return."

Constance hugged Eric, and the others came around, and group hugged. All in tears. Constance prayed for strength and healing, and that, as time passed, so would the pain of losing someone so meaningful and beautiful in their lives. For now, there were not enough words to ease the pain, so they chose to just be together and hurt together. Somehow their tears were cleansing and purging the beginning of their grief cycle they knew they'd each have to find their own way, but for this weekend, they would do it together.

On the way back to their childhood home, they stopped by the storage company nearby and bought fifty boxes, wide tape, and permanent markers so they could package and properly store valuables they wished to keep. Constance reminded Sandrida to please consider getting a box or two for Annabeth Marie so that she could have some of her personal belongings and some items to remember her mommy by.

Sandrida was such a remarkable thinker that she had already been making a list of items she felt were important to keep, even Elizabeth Marie's medical records, just in case something came up and she had to answer questions for whatever reason. She also wanted Constance to know how angry she was with their sister because she had no right to give their home to the bank. Their parents left the house to both, and Elizabeth Marie did a reverse mortgage without her knowledge, and it was just not fair that it was binding and legal and she had zero say in the matter. Still, she understood Elizabeth Marie's health had worsened, and she had to quit working. She and Annabeth Marie needed a place to live.

In this moment, Sandrida and Constance agreed to focus on right now. Looking for her vital documents was a priority. Constance had already discussed with all of them that Elizabeth Marie woke her up out of her sleep on the night she passed to let her know she wouldn't leave without speaking with her and giving her instructions on where to look for the documents she had hidden so that not just anyone could find and misuse her information. She knew Constance would go and look for her and find her paperwork amid the chaos. They would especially need her social security card, birth certificate, and driver's license.

On the day she entered the girls' childhood home, it was painfully thick with the spirit of death and loss. Constance had to sit down right away and catch her breath. Tears of deep grief overwhelmed her. Her boundless love for Elizabeth Marie and understanding that already Annabeth Marie had been removed from the home and placed into foster care was just more than Constance could sustain. Buckled over the nearest chair, Constance cried uncontrollably. When she saw Sandrida come over, they hugged each other, and just wept some more.

Sandrida whispered, "Constance, we have torn this house upside-down looking for her documents but can't find them anywhere. If you just want to skip doing this today, we can just go."

"No Sandrida. I already know where to go and look and find her stuff. I also know that our sister was a hoarder, and we have very little time to go through the rooms of this huge house to box up whatever you may wish to keep. We also need to bring out anything you want to sell so that you will have money to lay her down to rest, even if you just wish to cremate her and put her in a special container. We already know she wanted her ashes to go to each of us, her siblings, some to her beloved ocean, and some to her daughter. So, let's get started and just give me a little time to be in her personal restroom."

An hour later, after sorting material into throwaway piles, keep boxes, and garage sale stacks, Constance yelled for Sandrida to come and look. There on the counter, she had put the social security card, birth certificate, and driver's license.

Sandrida squealed. "Oh, my goodness. I promise you; we searched every inch of this bathroom and could not find anything except her medicines, jewelry, and a container of pandas and elephants she was obviously putting together to give away to family and her baby girl in anticipation of her death. Tell me Constance, where in the heck did you find them?"

Constance showed Sandrida a wide heavily taped large envelope with a message on it telling Constance to give the envelope to Sandrida and to share how much she loved all of us.

"Sandrida, it was right where she told me to look, taped up in an envelope attached to the inside of the cabinet where the sink is at. It was on the back end of the pipes taped to the rooftop." Looking in the cabinet alone, one would just overlook it. Sandrida just shook her head in disbelief.

"Here, Sandrida. You take this envelope and do what you have to do with the documents. She also left Annabeth Marie documents. You will need them for her therapies and school. Make sure you do not let anyone have this information. You will also need this information to obtain her death certificate, so store everything where only you have access as if your life depends on it."

After boxing up twenty-five boxes with what they wished to keep, Sandrida comes to where Constance is at and says, "Let's go home. I just can't be here any longer. It's too much, and I'm tired from crying so much and just need to get away. We can bring the twins tomorrow and box up more stuff. Anything that does not sell will be moved to my house, and we will try to have a garage sale over there as well. Constance, I just can't believe she came to you and told you goodbye and showed you where her vital documents were at. What was that like? That is something that would be in a movie, but it happened to you. That is truly incredible."

"To be honest, my gut was already mourning at the time of her death. I had received voicemails from Francisco to call him back, and finally, he left a message about her passing. I had already felt it in my spirit and did not want to pick up the phone. While asleep, I was woken by Elizabeth Marie. The whole corner of my bedroom was blazing with a hazy white light and a voice telling me to wake up; we had to talk. Our visit was probably about an hour long, with her giving me instructions about her documents to search for and us covering a huge number of memories through the years. We laughed and cried together, and then she said they were calling her, and she had to go.

'Tell my Annabeth Marie that I will always be right there by her side, and she can talk with me anywhere, any time. I love her always beyond the grave.'

"Sandrida, I remember just being bathed in tears and not wishing her to go, but just like she came, she was gone in an instant, and so was that bubble of space with the bright heavenly light. I have never experienced anything like it. I was left feeling exhausted, almost winded. I just went to sleep and slept deeply. When I woke up, it was like I was on a mission to come to Arizona."

The rest of the day was spent cooking, talking, and with the rest of the family. Amid pain, it was nice to just be together. The twins were the reason for smiling and laughing. They kept telling story after story about Elizabeth Marie and her ways. She was such a funny person, and they loved her so much. Keeping her alive by sharing her stories was what they planned to do forever because she is loved that much. She will never be forgotten, and she will always be a part of the family.

Leaving Arizona was tough because somehow it made Elizabeth Marie's death final. Constance believed that a part of her had died too, never to be whole again. Her best friend in life, her favorite sister, her love bond from early childhood, just gone. The chasm in her heart was endless, and she knew it would not ever be filled, yet it would be crucial to compartmentalize the pain and give to a higher power until the day they would reunite and be made whole again.

Chapter 17

Magdelina's Salem

Through the years, people have asked what it was like reuniting with Magdelina since we went through the most trauma prior to being a part of the childcare protective system and then adopted at a later age than most children. To be honest, Mami's prediction that I would not see Magdelina until after I was in my fifties came true. Life event after event occurred in such a way that financially blocked any opportunity to meet. Magdelina and I have had many conversations over the phone, hoping that we would be together prior to our deaths. Then it happened.

February 2023: a still small voice told me the time had come to see Magdelina, to finish my third book of my diary-turned-fiction series, and to complete a couple of other projects. I just laughed and thought, *"Lord, I give up and count on you to lead the way. You know what you are asking takes a lot of money that I don't have, and it also puts me in a predicament because you know that I won't be begging for money from anyone, just to go and complete these tasks."* Then, the voice showed me scripture that reprimanded me and had me rethink my attitude in silence. Looking in scripture at Isaiah 55: 8–9, it was there, just like I had heard. His thoughts are not my thoughts, and His ways are not my ways. The heavens are higher than the earth, so are the Lord's ways higher than my ways and His thoughts higher than my thoughts. I was immediately humbled and started to cry. I am so stubborn, and even though, over and over, the Lord has gotten me through some incredibly tough times, I still question His love and leadership. What an odd thing for me to do. As a child, I had become so disappointed in the adults that were supposed to protect me and raise me that, over time, all I knew to rely on was myself. Occasionally, a friend was put on my life path, but it was still tough to rely on the God of the Universe because He represented a father figure, and I had already learned those weren't trustworthy or genuinely caring of my needs and were never there to love and guide. Still, I listened to that still small voice, and I am learning to trust it with all my heart and soul.

Getting off the couch, my husband and I decided to go to the casino to observe people, relax, play on some slot machines, and have fun. I was thinking I had to play on the machine that I was instructed to play. Driving to the casino, I had doubts but when we arrived, it appeared winning was going to be a steady occurrence for me. Nothing big, just ten or twenty dollars here and there, but still winning. After a couple of hours playing, it was late and time to head home. It was a quarter till midnight, and we were both ready to go home. We were walking toward the exit, and I told my husband to stop with me at the Jerry Jones machines because they were the Dallas Cowboys football slot machines and were so much fun. *I never quit believing in our American Team!* We may not have won a Super Bowl in decades, but tonight could be the night we win here! How could I go wrong? I even had my number 11 jersey on, and it was a lucky one! I already knew this was the machine I was to play and win what was needed to do what the Lord had instructed me, but I still doubted that I would win anything. Nevertheless, I may as well finish out the night on this quarter machine and head home. On the third roll, the machine went haywire and kept on going with over twenty thousand quarters gleaming at me. My husband smiled and stated, "Those are not quarters. You better look again. Those are dollars." I looked at what I had played, and in small print, sure enough, I was playing on a dollar machine. Wow. I couldn't quit beaming with my mouth wide open in awe. I believe that I was in shock. Jerry Jones' machine had just paid me a little over twenty thousand dollars. No more excuses. This cash, after taxes, would allow me to pay down enough to complete the tasks that I was to complete this year.

I immediately called Magdelina and told her that I was coming to visit over Labor Day weekend if she was ready for me to visit. She didn't come out and say that she'd believe it when she saw it, but she did say, "Hopefully, before I die, we can see each other in person."

"No, Magdelina. I am telling you. I will be there for a long weekend this Labor Day weekend, so let's begin planning on everything we want to see and do. Truthfully, I want to see your daily routines and meet the people you speak of from your weekly activities, like your everyday visits to Dunkin' Donuts, where you get your coffee. I also want to go to Salem, a beach, and maybe drive around to see the landscaping of your area."

We were both so excited about the possibility of our dream coming true—about seeing one another in person—that it just seemed unreal.

"I will get with my daughters, and we will have stuff to do by the time that you get here and of course, you will stay with me. I must move some furniture around and redo my stacks of clothing so that everything looks nice and neat, but I have time to sort it out before you arrive. You know, in my spirit, I know this is the year that we will see each other."

Week after week from then on, we were planning and wishing on places to visit, food to eat, anything we must see together, spending time with her two gorgeous daughters and son-in-law, and talking about anything we wanted to exchange from now and our preceding life encounters.

The day came when I was up in the clouds, and I couldn't believe I was on the way to see Magdelina. I just couldn't quit thinking that it had been forty-four long years since we had seen one another. Surreal. How I have missed my sister and longed for a big sister to grow up with. Surely, the stars have aligned, and our Father in heaven has seen to it that it was time for us to be together in person. Even though my flight was over an hour late landing, everything was in slow motion as my ride stopped in front of her home. I saw her coming around the corner of a large two-story Victorian house, but it was too dark to see the details of the house. Magdelina was still shorter than me but appeared so tall and proud, at this moment, to see me.

Walking toward each other, never taking our eyes off one another, we just kept sharing a connection that no one would ever understand and take from us. Eyes misting, we hugged for a very long time. It felt good to reconnect. Peace and closure. Full circle at last. To each our own. Lost in our thoughts and soul searches, we feel a resounding elation of love, goodness, and sisterhood with a bloodline that has kept us connected through decades. Misted over eyes now turned into a surge of silent tears. Even though no words were uttered, our messages to one another were bountiful and willingly received. It's like we already knew what each one of us was thinking.

Out of nowhere, Magdelina snapped us out of our historical trance, and she was laughing for us to go to her apartment up in the attic of this house. For the first time in decades, she was extremely tired and sleepy, which is unusual for her because she rarely sleeps.

"Look at me, Magdelina, tonight you shall sleep. The spell is broken, us seeing one another. Our past haunted spells are broken. Every one of them. Do you hear me? In your closet of ghosts, you will no longer need to stay awake and draw attention to protect us younger ones. You no longer must be on the lookout. No one is left to ever hurt us again. You are released, free to rest, and have your own life now. Tonight, you sleep and soundly relax."

Magdelina is wide-eyed. "You don't understand. My therapist has given me medicines forever and they can't even make me sleep longer than thirty minutes."

"Magdelina, you will see. Don't worry."

After a full night's slumber, we were up at the crack of dawn, going to Magdelina's favorite coffee shop. She woke up in disbelief, awed at the fact that she had slept for hours and not her usual thirty minutes and could not even recall any of her haunting dreams.

She was explaining everything in her world was within a five-mile radius. She could grocery shop, eat out, get her daily coffee, get her hair cut, nails painted, and be entertained any time she wanted. She was in a safe and friendly neighborhood, and she loved her town. Her nickname at the donut shop was Mama Dunks and she had a well-established crew of caring friends that met her daily to chat and spend time together. It was easy to see why she considered the Salem area her own.

Once breakfast was finished, we were picked up by her beautiful girls and kept on exploring the tourist side of Salem. Meeting her daughters was dreamlike, with a source of pride to see offspring that are kind, loving, and immensely intelligent. We walked throughout downtown, ate to our hearts' content, and learned all the history through the eyes of my family. They were experts of their hometown, knowing hidden boutiques and back stories of historical locations and so many specifics beyond just the regular tourist trap sites. The whole experience was thrilling, adventurous, and just worth coming back to again. The closeness that I experienced and felt for my nieces, nephew, and sister blessed me beyond expression. Plans to reconnect started for the next time visit.

Chapter 18

Sister Chat

Reconnecting with Magdelina, she wanted to make sure that we had focused time to sister chat about some deep secrets that only we knew the particularities of. So we waited until the end of the day, right before we fell asleep, to cover some topics that were heavy on our hearts.

"Constance, in all the times that I was being chased to be beaten by our insane—I refuse to call her grandmother—it never occurred to me that you were in the other room, having to deal with molestation. I thought I was the only one being hurt, and it did not matter if they left the rest of you alone. My question for you is, how do you survive the pain of relentless whippings and mental abuse?"

"Magdelina, truthfully, all I can tell you is that I had to forgive the past and accept that I wasn't responsible for poor adult choices. I don't like what they did to us or how those who knew about it handled the situation by staying out of it. I told myself, as an adult, I could leave that to the past and create my own world, which I have. I have also gone back on my visits to ensure no one else is being abused and I teach the children what to say and how to reach out if they are in danger. Also, every day, I must choose to be happy, productive, and mentally in a good place. Naturally, I tend to be negative and realistic in my thinking and I often must make a choice to be overly optimistic or I can go to that deep, dark place of hate, resentment and self-pity. Each day, I choose the positive and strive for active living that has purpose in taking joy in the small things. Then, I allow myself to process unpleasant thoughts and feelings, giving myself time and grace to be human. I learned long ago that I don't have to be the caregiver, nor do I have to stand up and take responsibility for anything that is not my business. The hard part was accepting I don't have to be perfect, I don't owe anyone anything for my existence, and I don't have to do all the work to be acceptable. I can just be me, sit in silence and allow the world to move on without me, and that is alright, too. What about you, sister? How do you survive?"

"I was lucky to have very patient parents who adopted me and spent a lot of time getting me the therapy and help I needed, and God knows that was an extensive amount in the beginning of my stay with them. Dealing with me was a lot of work, but they stuck with me. My dad had learned how to handle me with his college studies, and both were so patient with me. They also allowed me the opportunity and time to adjust. I had to learn to be a child, for example, and to accept my room was my room. The toys that were given to me were my toys, and I could play with them, and they would not be taken from me. My mom cried when I was finally able to tell her that I loved her because it took a very long time for me to feel safe enough to say that I loved her. They taught me that my feelings were mine and I could keep them. So, to this day, I don't forgive my abusers, and that includes what we call our maternal grandmother. I can't help what happened to her in her childhood. It didn't give her the right to hurt us as an adult. Plus, why should I forgive someone who was sorry about beating us one day, and then would apologize, but the next day she would whip us again and not just beat us but torture us until we bled, and our skin was gutted, until chunks of deeper skin was ripped exposing blood and fat. That isn't being sorry. I will never forgive her, and I am good with that. I know what I know, and she does not deserve my forgiveness or empathy. Constance, I am not you. I can't just forgive the injustice that exists now or was. There is no excuse for abuse, and especially hurting the innocent who rely on adults for care and protection."

"Magdelina, I forgive. I don't justify their behaviors, which were unacceptable, and I don't forget. That is why I don't go out of my way to visit them in their old age because they need help or comfort and forgiveness now. Nope they can rot in a nursing home or just live their lives out alone. I don't care, nor do I owe them anything just because they grow old or get a conscious or find Jesus, for that matter. I value my time and choose to share it with those that truly care for me and love me."

"May she rot in a very special place in hell for those who abuse God's little children. I am grown now, and I have a voice. If she were alive, I'd be all up in her face telling her about herself, and I would protect myself completely, she wouldn't ever be able to harm another child ever, not under my watch. I would make sure she'd never even get to be around my children. I don't care that she could cast spells that came true. I believe that I can cast them also, and there is power in numbers, so you and I could have ganged up on her had we been able to cast a spell when we were children."

"Magdelina, did I ever tell you how she died?"

"Tell me, sister, and I hope it was brutal."

"Honestly, Magdelina, I understand your pain, but no one, not even my worst enemy, deserves to die like this. You know there is a myth in our family history that says if you choose to practice the gift of knowledge, healing, and bringing back the dead, then you will die young. We are doomed to die by water or fire."

"Hold up, sister. By gift, are you talking about how we can see or hear the dead, tell the future, or just sense what is going on in the present or future?"

"Yes, Magdelina, I don't care if you call it shamanism, witchcraft, voodoo, black magic, fortune telling, spiritual healing, or whatever. It is the fact that you tapped into the supernatural to find out information, change a destination, or heal someone to extend their life here on earth. I shall send you the write-up on her story because it made the news. She was at the ranch, cooking outside, like they do up in Hill Country where the wild thistles grow. On that day she had built a good-sized fire and was setting up her pots for a long day of stirring up her stews. Generally, she wore her vividly flowered pants and wild flamboyant tops, but on that date, she wore a very old simple, thin, long, cotton dress. As she was whipping around to pick up and toss in some more chopped wood in the fire, the edge of her dress caught on fire. Because her dress was so old, it rapidly engulfed her in flames. She was screaming so loud when our Uncle Vino was driving toward her house. He quickly went inside the house to grab a blanket and went back to wrap it around her. He later told me that he had paused for a second because of her cruelty to her children. He wanted her to die a painful death, but now that it was here, all he could think of is that this was his mom, and he had to save her. Once he wrapped her in the blanket, he dropped her to the ground, telling her to roll. He had managed to put out the fire and yell to his cousin to call the ambulance quickly because she was burned badly. Tio Vino said he couldn't even recognize her. Her hair had caught fire, and she had passed out from the pain, or he thought she was dead. It didn't take long before a helicopter was there to fly her to the nearest hospital with a burns victim unit."

"Oh my god, Constance. I have not ever heard of this story. Then what happened?"

"Magdelina, they tried everything they could possibly attempt, but her burns were beyond what they could do for her. If only she had known to stop, drop, and roll over like they teach you in school now in case of something like this, maybe she would have had a fighting chance. They say once they got her to the hospital, she did not last long. She died from complications of her extensive burn wounds and smoke inhalation. It was an excruciating, agonizing death. Honestly, I hope that I die in my sleep. I can't imagine something this traumatic. You and I both know she was the one who actively practiced her spells. People came from all over just to be healed or cast incantations on others and pay for her to sum up the dead. She was doomed to expire young. Still, I cringe at the thought of how she died."

"Constance, I agree that no one deserves to die such a painful death, but she got karma, and that was on her. If she had chosen the path of being a loving, caring person then surely her death would have been more forgiving. Nothing happens without a reason, and she created her own destiny by choosing revenge and meanness. I do not feel sorry for her, nor do I choose to ever forgive her brutality to her own blood—her children and grandchildren."

"Magdelina, don't you find it ironic that everyone outside of the family loved her and never knew how wicked she was behind closed doors? Why is that? Our own godmother insists she was the sweetest, gentlest soul she ever knew, and she was one of the best cooks in the neighborhood. She would share with anyone. Our Mami and she were known for throwing some of the best neighborhood block parties around. Explain that to me because it just does not make sense to me."

Magdelina exclaims, "We are not meant to know some things in this lifetime, but all shall be revealed when time ends and our Lord returns. The only explanation is that this world belongs to evil and his troops, and we wrestle not against flesh and blood but a spiritual warfare, and we must move forward with a good fight. My sister, we have fought a good fight and been blessed to have moved beyond that way of living. I am grateful for that."

"Yes, Magdelina. We are free to be unrestricted and choose a different path than our childhood prison of pain. We can choose goodness and follow the path of caring and giving. See, we are here together at last."

We hug each other, smile and laugh together.

"Sister, we both have a voice and we can use it to help ourselves and help others. Yes, we are free! I love you."

"And I love you. You know, I am so grateful for the telephone and now social media so that we can keep up with each other. The Lord willing, we will see each other again. I have yet to discover why we can't seem to be blessed financially. I just know that we are supposed to be in a better position financially, and I am open to receiving our blessings. Let's pray that we may see each other again in this lifetime and more than one more time! Good night and get some more well-deserved sleep."

"I love you too, and tomorrow we must cook and celebrate us together."

After this trip to see Magdelina, it was clear that the third book of the series would most likely write itself. Constance knew what would take the most time for the ending of the book, and it was mostly because she never wanted to let go of Elizabeth Marie, but the time had come to free her spirit so that she would fully move on to eternity until it was time to meet again.

Chapter 19

Finally Free

Constance knew after her trip to visit Magdelina that the time had come to set Elizabeth Marie's spirit to move forward with her life ever after, even though it is difficult to let go of hearing her voice as she has joined in with her stories to share her side of her thoughts for this third book, based on real events in my diary, and stored up memories. All has come to a point to be at peace with the past. It's been twelve years since her death, and grief is never-ending, but somehow, it goes to its healing place, and all that remains are, periodically, moments of loss and pain. Replacing the void after facing and processing emotions of loss, anger, and deep sorrow are focused memories of her legacy and goodness, celebrating a short life well lived. Elizabeth Marie is forever one of the most important people that has ever been a part of my life, and her laughter, endless stories, and jokes will forever live on. Her extension of life breathes on through Annabeth Marie, and DNA extended to heritage.

Decades of choosing to live life to the fullest and sharing Mami's messages has allowed for each of her children to free themselves to focus on their positives. Constance knows in her heart that with the release of this story comes her restoration of what should have been. She is open and ready for anything coming her way and embraces success, goodness, love, positiveness, and the freedom of daily living. Her desire now is to travel, to have a home to call her own, to complete her education, and to publish the rest of the books stored in her soul. Her purpose in life of sharing her Mami's request of a few family stories with the world is fulfilled, and now onto living in the moment.

Where Are They Now?

- *Mami* celebrates beyond the living that her children are free to live their best lives, and their historical chronicles will not be in vain. May the American family be restored.

- *Papi* or *Freddy* made peace with his past and his children. Flying past my left ear were a pair of red cardinals, who then landed on the rooftop of a house. They were perched there singing toward me as if to say, "We are at peace, we are together. and we will always watch over you." Then my eyes watered as they flew into the horizon as if to say, 'We are free at last.'

- *Magdelina* resides on the East Coast near her two gorgeous daughters that she is most fond of and proud to call her own. Every day, she is grateful to live a good life freed of her past. She takes joy in having been adopted by the best parents ever, and as an adult, she is truly aware of what they did for her and how they taught her what love and a healthy home should look like.

- *Francisco* is doing well. He found spirituality and has taken joy in his faith and family. He travels often to Hill Country to spend time with Mami's cousin, who raised him and who he considers a mother figure to him. Francisco loves to ride his motorcycle and travels through the hills of Texas.

- *Baby girl/Federica* laid to rest at three months. This child blessed our family with love and laughter. Gone but never forgotten.

- *Sandrida* lives in the desert and loves being with her family. She revolves her world around her children and grandchildren and is grateful for her life. Any given day, you will find her in her kitchen, cooking from scratch delicious Mexican meals and salsas.

- *Elizabeth Marie* is so proud of her daughter and is grateful for the family who took her in. Even in death, love has no chains that bind it, she watches over her greatest gift and joy, her daughter. All around as the wind, rain, rolling waves of the ocean, the lullaby of the wildflowers of the meadows, and the vast spread of the heavenly stars, her love is endless toward her child and family.

- *Romando* resides in Arizona and enjoys the outdoors and skateboarding. He lives a simple life and continues to work toward independent living. He is happy being near his supportive family and church to keep his nights and weekend full of activities.

- *Constance* continues to reside in Texas, researching family history, and takes pleasure visiting relatives and friends. You will find her engaged with loved ones, cooking and baking for them, and traveling. Those closest to her know her passion for her four-legged fur babies and will find her meandering the great outdoors, enjoying the sunshine, trees, and, whenever possible, the crashing waves of the ocean on the beaches of many sandy coasts of America. *Constance* will soon release her first nonfiction, a book of thirteen essentials to childcare regulatory compliance success.

- *Tio Petro* lost his battle to cancer but watches over his amazing wife and children, ever proud of the goodness his family shares with their world.

- *Marisa* and *Constance* stay in touch by phone, social media, text, and in person. Sister friends for a lifetime. Anytime is a good time for conversation. Morning, noon, and night, whether it is to share the latest great event in our lives or a bummer event, we enjoy moments with each other. Marisa is semi-retired and enjoys traveling, gardening, and spending time with her family.

Those wishing to connect with Connie A. Thompson, author of:

- *THERE ARE: NO SECRETS* (Also available as an audiobook)
- *LOST CHILDREN WHERE THE WILD THISTLES GROW*
- *HOW HIGH DO CHIGGERS JUMP IN THIS MOMENT CALLED LIFE?* (Soon to be an audiobook)

Coming soon:

- *GOT IT! UNPREPARED NO MORE*

can visit her by email at connieathompson01@gmail.com

About the Author

Connie A. Thompson, author of:

- *THERE ARE: NO SECRETS*
- *HOW HIGH DO CHIGGERS JUMP IN THIS MOMENT CALLED LIFE?*
- *LOST CHILDREN WHERE THE WILD THISTLES GROW*

Connie A. Thompson was educated at Emporia State University, Kansas, lives in Texas, and is grateful for the joys of everyday living. Connie hopes that by writing about her own experiences, she will promote and cheer on American families to pursue and preserve healthy relationships.

You may find Connie connecting with her friends and family and loving on her fur babies.

LOST CHILDREN WHERE THE WILD THISTLES GROW is Connie's third novel, personal diary-turned-fiction, in a series of three. *GOT IT! UNPREPARED NO MORE* will be her first nonfiction—available soon.

Made in the USA
Monee, IL
10 January 2025